EAGLES
OF
DESTINY
...a Prophetic Concept

BY DR. ALAN PATEMAN

BY DR. JENNIFER PATEMAN

AVAILABLE FROM **APMI** PUBLICATIONS,
AMAZON.COM AND OTHER RETAIL OUTLETS

*E*AGLES OF *D*ESTINY

...a Prophetic Concept

DR. ALAN PATEMAN
The Holy Spirit is BECKONING!

But they that wait upon the Lord shall renew their strength; they shall mount up with wings as eagles; they shall run, and not be weary; and they shall walk, and not faint.

(Isaiah 40:31)

BOOK TITLE:
Eagles of Destiny …*a Prophetic Concept*

WRITTEN BY Dr. ALAN PATEMAN
Paperback ISBN: 978-1-909132-20-7
Hardcover ISBN: 978-1-909132-22-1
eBook ISBN: 978-1-909132-21-4

Published By:
APMI Publications
In Partnership with Truth for the Journey Books **52**
Email: publications@alanpateman.com
www.AlanPatemanMinistries.com

Acknowledgements:
Author/Design/Senior Editor/Publisher: Apostle Dr. Alan Pateman
Editing/Proofreading/Research: Dr. Jennifer Pateman
Computer Administration/Office Manager: Dr. Dorothea Struhlik
Cover Image Credit: www.wallpapercave.com

Unless otherwise indicated, all scriptural quotations are from the King James Version of the Bible.

*Where scriptures appear with special emphasis (**in bold,** italic or <u>underlined</u>) we have edited them ourselves in order to bring focused attention within the context of this subject being taught.*

❖

Dedication

I lovingly dedicate this book to all of our LICU students around the world.

Remember, a life given to true revelation will always demonstrate the Spirit's power so that faith and the faith of others will not rest upon man's wisdom but on God's supernatural power that brings freedom and liberty into every situation.

❖

Table of Contents

Introduction

I
t is with great pleasure that I am able to bring this book "Eagles of Destiny, a Prophetic Concept" to you my dear friends and encourage you to reach for the heights like an eagle, to ride on the currents of the Holy Spirit and go where He desires to carry you.

The vision to write a book on eagles relating to a NEST and then travelling out from it all over the world is something God spoke to me about many years ago. In fact I bought a large trophy *(in 1998)* with an eagle mounted on the top and an inscription that said: Alan Pateman Ministries International – Flying out to and fro from the Eagles Nest, Italy.

Then again more recently in 2013 the Lord spoke to me again about emphasising on the eagle and its need for the right food for the journey and the importance of the nest!

We need to know where we can be fed, belong, be mentored, supported and encouraged; the nest is such a place!

I hope you are part of a Nest were you can take flight as God intended. Your life and journey is too important to give to chance. God has a destiny for you that you must prepare for. He is not the author of confusion but of righteousness, faith, love and peace. That amazing peace will flood your life, once you realise that at last you are in the midst of the perfect will of God.

Then you will be able to face the challenges, knowing that He is with you and has an exciting plan for your life and future.

For many years I've been travelling throughout the nations and found that many are struggling and scratching on the ground like turkeys rather than overcoming and being successful like the eagle who is depicted in scripture.

Our perceptions of ourselves are not always as God sees us. **"FOR AS HE THINKS IN HIS HEART, SO IS HE"** *(Proverbs 23:7 AMPC).* But we must start seeing ourselves as God sees us and not as we see ourselves.

> *There we saw the… giants… and **we were in our own sight as grasshoppers,** and so we were in their sight.*
> *(Numbers 13:33 AMPC)*

Prophetic not Parochial

We need sight for the journey and we need sight for the future. We MUST see ourselves as God sees us and have prophetic vision. The Proverbs 31 Woman *(representing the Church, The Bride of Christ)* had prophetic vision. It says, "Clothed in strength and dignity, with nothing to fear, she SMILES WHEN SHE THINKS ABOUT THE FUTURE" *(Proverbs 31:25 VOICE).*

> *Strength and dignity are her clothing and her position is strong and secure; SHE REJOICES OVER THE FUTURE [THE LATTER DAY or time to come, knowing that she and her family are in READINESS for it]!*
> *(Proverbs 31:25 AMPC)*

A spiritual eagle lives in READINESS. Always waiting, watching, preparing and learning. Seeing into the future, projecting. Eagles go forwards. Never back. They have long distant vision. They are not short sighted or parochial. We must start living NOW, as God intended.

"The eye of the eagle is very curious. It has something like an inner eyelid, only it is very thin; and the eagle can draw this over its eye, like a curtain, whenever there is too much light.

You have heard perhaps that it can look directly at the bright sun; and this is the reason. It can see a great deal farther than we can; and when it is very high in the air, so that it would look to you but little larger than a speck, it often sees some small animal on the ground and flies down to catch it."[1]

Some years ago God gave me a mandate to go through the nations and raise up an army of warriors *(eagles)* for the end times, for the glory of the Lord.

At times, this seems rather militant. But as we look at the news it's not difficult to realise that the end times are upon us. We need right concepts and right Kingdom perspectives – more now than ever before.

Revelation Knowledge

AS EAGLES WE MUST FEED ON REVELATION KNOWLEDGE. THE RIGHT SEEDS PRODUCE THE RIGHT HARVEST. Let me just say, we are raising up thousands of eagles around the world, through the prophetic teaching and insights that this ministry brings.

APMI has various arms of ministry, such as the popular teaching series called, **"Truth for the Journey"** that goes out across the Internet each and every week without fail. Such articles are a *MUST* read for *every* prophetic eagle!

Also by way of preparation for life's intrepid journey, God has given and provided, **"LIFESTYLE INTERNATIONAL CHRISTIAN UNIVERSITY" – (LICU),** which is **the teaching arm** of Alan Pateman Ministries. I won't hold back by saying that this university will impact your life in a very real way. We have seen thousands of lives changed.

Then also as an Apostolic and Prophetic ministry, I travel to other Nests around the world where other eaglets desire to be fed!

A life given to true revelation will always demonstrate the Spirit's power so that our faith and the faith of others will not rest upon man's wisdom but on God's supernatural power that brings freedom and liberty into every situation.

Let's rise up and become all that God intended and encourage one another to fulfil the race.

Apostle Dr Alan Pateman

CHAPTER 1

Birds of a Feather Stick Together

Solitary and Territorial

Eagles can appear to be quite solitary and territorial birds, and can be found flying alone at high altitudes. Nevertheless they can be sociable when certain seasons dictate, but only with their own kind! Especially true in winter when eagles migrate and gather together into groups, to nest and hunt beside waterways that aren't frozen over and where the food supplies are more abundant. *(But this is largely governed by food supply. Eagles are territorial and don't generally flock like the vultures do).*

So eagles can and will be sociable but only during seasonal intervals and only with their own kind. Not with the sparrows, ravens, pigeons or other small birds, as no other bird can reach the altitudes that an eagle can.

Don't Conform to the Culture

In 2 Corinthians it states clearly that we too should stick with our own kind. Just as the eagle doesn't come down to a low level, nor should we.

BE YE NOT UNEQUALLY YOKED TOGETHER with unbelievers: for what fellowship hath righteousness with unrighteousness? And what communion hath light with darkness?

(2 Corinthians 6:14)

Even so, I can already hear the counterblast: "Well that's not very loving!" Nonetheless, light and dark don't mix. They never have and never will, *no matter how politically correct you want to make it!*

There is already too much mixture in the world *(people are desperate to get away from the confusion in their lives)*. So in answer to that - let me ask another question: If God is not the author of confusion, then who is? And how then can we actively partake in, enable or support confusion *(on any level)*?

GOD IS NOT THE AUTHOR OF CONFUSION, BUT OF <u>PEACE</u>...

(1 Corinthians 14:33)

People will always want you to come down to their level and when you won't, therein lays the separation. *"Come out from among them and be ye SEPARATE"* (2 Corinthians 6:17). Even if you don't separate yourself, people will begin to separate themselves from you, especially when you don't conform to the woke culture!

Instead of being pulled down by what that culture dictates, rise up and soar like an eagle, who is always most comfortable in the heavens. You too are born for the same!

So here's what I want you to do, God helping you: Take your everyday, ordinary life – your sleeping, eating, going-to-work, and walking-around life – and place it before God as an offering. Embracing what God does for you is the best thing you can do for him.

Don't become so well-adjusted to your culture that you fit into it without even thinking. Instead, **FIX YOUR ATTENTION ON GOD.** *You'll be changed from the inside out. Readily recognize what he wants from you, and quickly respond to it.*

UNLIKE THE CULTURE AROUND YOU, ALWAYS DRAGGING YOU DOWN TO ITS LEVEL OF IMMATURITY, *God brings the best out of you, develops well-formed maturity in you.*

(Romans 12:2 MSG)

Turkeys and Eagles

In my formative years, I grew up on the farm, in fact many different farms, as my father was a farm-hand *(labourer)* and we travelled and lived from one farm to another. We had a large family with seven other siblings, and all grew up experiencing the freedom of life on a farm. I have good memories of those days and sad ones too.

The main sadness was in the area of my education or the lack thereof. By moving so many times during my early school life *(incredibly 20 different schools!)* it did not afford any of us a good education, to say the least.

In fact at the age of 27 I still could not read or write and suffered with severe dyslexia. These were indeed disadvantages, but God used them for His Glory and developed a passion in my heart to help people all over the world; to reach true potential, especially those who lack the opportunity in the area of education.

Today I am the founder and president of an international network of universities *(LICU)*, i.e. *"one university in different locations."* Something impossible for someone like me and yet God intervened and did the impossible!

Perception is Everything

My experiences have helped shape who I am today and quite frankly God has never permitted me the luxury of identifying myself as one of life's victims! Perception is everything; I noticed this as a child, while watching the birds of the air that lived on the farm.

In particular I noticed the difference between chickens, turkeys and eagles. Not that we ever had eagles on our farm! But we would see many hawks going after the field mice and revel in the sight. It was exciting to watch how precise they were.

Eagles were rare sightings but fascinated my young imagination because they were even greater than the impressive hawk.

Clumsy & Easily Satisfied!

I remember feeding our turkeys with boiled potato peals, including what we called the slops *(waste)*. They were satisfied with this!

Turkeys are not meat eaters. Not raptors. Nor hunters. They didn't like the fresh meat of the Word *(spiritually speaking)* and were easily satisfied with slops!

I noticed too how the chickens and turkeys were much the same in their mentality and behaviour. They were small-minded and short-sighted; content with grovelling for seeds and grains and what was in front of them. Secure in being grounded and never seemed to strive for flight but were content in their close surroundings.

The eagle however was built for long distance flight and had amazing vision. His scope *(mentality/behaviour)* was illustrious and his abilities far outweighed those of his counterparts.

In all fairness turkeys can actually fly. Many people consider them as grounded birds. However they aren't entirely. On our farm, they got airborne on rare occasions, emergencies only and without achieving any significant heights!

Reluctant & Underdeveloped

I grew up believing that turkeys were such reluctant flyers due to the fact that they were lazy and had underdeveloped wings for being out of practice!

23

This speaks volumes when we mirror this up against the lives of believers who might live their lives in a similar way, always reluctant and unwilling to go for the Lord *(see Isaiah 1:19)*. In the end they are awkward, underdeveloped and clumsy, again spiritually speaking. What a sad outcome. God wants so much more for us:

> **LOOK AT THE BIRDS OF THE AIR;** *they neither sow nor reap nor gather into barns, and yet your heavenly Father keeps feeding them.* **ARE YOU NOT WORTH MUCH MORE THAN THEY?**
>
> *(Matthew 6:26 AMPC)*

> **LOOK AT THE BIRDS,** *free and unfettered, not tied down to a job description, careless in the care of God. And* **YOU COUNT FAR MORE TO HIM THAN BIRDS.**
>
> *(MSG)*

For me, the turkey and the chicken were such common birds. With nothing remarkable about them, compared to the hawk and especially the eagle that is in a class of its own!

The Holy Spirit Beckoning

An eagle certainly does not live off of slops or boiled potato peals. He is a predator and not dependent on humans *(unless raised in captivity)*. He is a territorial and independent hunter, swift as the wind and agile, graceful to watch and never clumsy or awkward.

In such an environment as the farm, an eagle would never have been satisfied. The skies would be beckoning and he would instinctively know that there was more to life!

Many believers are like this. They go to churches where they cannot grow or develop, as they should. They are dissatisfied but don't know why. They feel guilty even, for not being as easily satisfied as everyone else. **But nothing quells the desire to soar! It's the Holy Spirit beckoning.**

Like the eagle, young believers instinctively yearn to soar and glide. NOT grovelling, earth-bound like common fowl.

Your wings are made for flight and powerful aerodynamics.

CHAPTER 2

Unyielding Vision

Eyes Designed for Distance

Eagles posses very keen vision, with eyes specially designed for long distance and precision. Eagles can focus on their prey from five kilometres away, which is over three miles! Once he narrows his focus, he goes after his prey with mind-blowing accuracy.

Accuracy because he not only has to calculate the height, speed and distance *(between him and his moving target),* he must also calculate the changing position and velocity of his escaping prey. This is ingenious and involves some major mathematical exactitude!

Throughout scripture there are references to the eagle. Not only must we have great ability to see clearly like the eagle *(spiritually)*, but must also have a clear VISION from God, which always looks impossible in the natural!

A vision that is genuinely from God, will always take more than the arm of the flesh to manage and fulfil it. In addition and essential to fulfilling any vision - is not taking your eye off the ball! Not being deterred from our mission or from finishing what God instructed us to do.

Hunger is the Best Motivator

The eagles lock target and don't quit till they achieve. If they miss, they try again. They go the distance and don't give up easily.

Concerning motivation, I recently watched a basketball coaching video, which my son posted on his Facebook page. The video was inspirational and very well put together, entitled: **"Fail Harder."** Inferring that all success is preceded by failure, using the slogan: *"New Philosophy: Fail Harder Now. Succeed Easier Later."*[2]

For our son, it was brilliant. Great slogan. Great delivery. Except, there's nothing *new* about failure coming before success. It has always been the case!

While the maker of the video thought his philosophy was something new, I would say there is nothing new about it! Finding a modern way of spinning, presenting or articulating an old philosophy doesn't make it new! Everything in life has always involved a process: of time, effort and progression.

Still I do agree that motivation is a *big deal* and key to most activities, in all our lives. The eagle is no less motivated, but what motivates the eagle? **Hunger with expectation. Always!**

Hope, a Partner of Faith

Now faith is the substance (hupostasis) of things hoped for, the evidence of things not seen.

(Hebrews 11:1)

Faith without expectation or hunger isn't faith, it's hope. By itself hope doesn't arrive anywhere far! And without faith it enjoys no under-guarding or support. Hope alone lacks all confidence; therefore hope and faith must remain indispensable partners.

While Hope is the visionary Faith is the substance; Faith creates *(gives substance to)* what Hope sees! Therefore our hope must be fixed on the promises of God and what He has already given us *(Hebrews 10:35; 3:6, 1 John 5:14)*.

This Hope, Faith with expectation is our assurance-confidence, concrete! **Our hunger for the Lord** *(not selfish ambition)* **should be our drive every single day.**

The Energy of Fresh Meat

It's true to say, the eagle can't go a day without considering hunting. Although physiologically speaking he doesn't need to eat every day, he still cannot run the risk of losing his energy for the next hunt. So either way, he must eat. He literally can't take a day off! The world won't stop spinning, for any of us to get off!

This again is true for the spiritual eagle, which also can't afford *(even consider)* to backslide and must search out revelation *(the fresh meat is God's Rhema Word)* daily, in order to keep up his or her spiritual strength.

So, if spiritual hunger is our motivator, what then should we hunger besides God's Word? RIGHTEOUSNESS, *(right living and right standing/relationship with God Himself)*. Scripture tells us that righteousness is what truly satisfies, therefore we must hunger *and* thirst for it:

> *Blessed are they which do* **hunger and thirst after RIGHTEOUSNESS:** *for they shall be filled.*
> > *(Matthew 5:6)*

> *Blessed* **and** *fortunate* **and** *happy* **and** *spiritually prosperous (in that state in which the born-again child of God enjoys His favor and salvation) are those who* **hunger and thirst for RIGHTEOUSNESS (UPRIGHTNESS AND RIGHT STANDING WITH GOD), FOR THEY SHALL BE COMPLETELY SATISFIED!**
> > *(Matthew 5:6 AMPC)*

Locked Focus

> *A double minded man is unstable in all his ways.*
> > *(James 1:8)*

Once an eagle locks target, he will not be deterred by anything. No obstacle is able to dissuade him from his focus. We too must have such locked focus, that no obstacle can unlock. Only then, like the eagle, will we succeed in reaching our goal.

But our focus, above all else is God Himself. He is our vision. Our goal. Our destiny. Our future. Our deliverance. Our salvation.

Many Changes Many Questions

Personally, I have been through so many changes and I have had so many questions in regards to the journey that I have been on. But His ways are not our ways. I too have been frustrated because of the lack of travelling opportunities, *(invitations)*. Although of course, Covid-19 has seemingly impacted so much Church activity. Even so, God is still in control of our lives.

I have spent years in different caves, sometimes for months at a time, but I have never wasted those precious moments. Books were developed, including vast teaching materials. What seemed to be times of obscurity, was in fact preparation for all that God had planed for my life.

Now, with the development of apostolic teaching centres, called LICU University Campuses, which also include correspondence studies, I reach more people and have more affect on the Body of Christ than I ever did rushing from one place to another. My biggest cry over the years, was for God to give me revelation and wisdom.

Sometimes I failed because I looked at others to see what they were doing; becoming a little jealous or bitter even. But the truth is we can learn from others, but we can't wear their armour. God is not going to do exactly the same thing through us – although some characteristics might be similar.

If we don't practice His presence daily, *(becoming increasingly accustomed to and intimate with the anointing, as we worship Him in Spirit and in truth, hungry to hear His voice),* everything else besides is a waste of time and subject to mere religious sentiments.

Many years ago, someone gave me a card, which at the time I assumed was an invitation but was disappointed to discover it simply stated: "LET GO AND LET GOD!" I must admit, that it has taken me nearly three decades to come even remotely close to realising that goal!

We all have to make Jesus more important than who we think we are. The world needs Jesus more than an apostle. Whatever accolades follow you; it doesn't matter, what matters most is that He is being lifted up. That all men come to know Him and that we preach a simple gospel of love and salvation, where we lay hands on those who are sick and cast out demons.

To serve Him, is the intention of our locked focus.

CHAPTER 3

Living Prophetically

God Wants to Communicate

Our God is a personal God. "He desires intimate fellowship with individuals more than a distant relationship with humanity as a race. When Adam and Eve were the entire race, the Almighty walked and talked with them. But ever since sin dulled human ears to hearing and human eyes to seeing God, He has not been able to communicate with everyone individually.

The race *(humanity)* as a whole does not desire His fellowship and is not sensitive enough to hear His voice. Although the coming of the Holy Spirit, the birth of the Church, and the writing of the Bible did not eliminate the need for the prophetic voice of the Lord; in fact, it intensified that need."

Jesus declared in Acts 1:5: *"...in a few days you will be baptized with the Holy Spirit."*

Jesus was speaking here about the baptism of the Holy Spirit. He said it was an empowering for supernatural service for Him. This is something more than the inner life with Him that is available through the new birth. The baptism in the Spirit is the power of God equipping the believer for supernatural service.

Peter goes on to say in *(Acts 2:17),* that the prophet Joel was speaking of the Church age when he proclaimed, "I will pour out my Spirit in those days, and your sons and daughters shall prophesy."

Paul emphasized that truth when he told the church at Corinth to "covet to prophesy" *(1 Corinthians 14:39; Ephesians 4:11).*

"God still wants the revelations of His will to be vocalized. So He has established the prophetic ministry as a voice of revelation and illumination, which will reveal the mind of Christ to the human race. He also uses this ministry to give specific instructions to individuals concerning His personal will for their lives."[3]

Prophets are known in scripture as **SEERS**. Even the testimony of our Lord is prophetic *("the spirit of prophecy")* and while we might not all be prophets in the Body of Christ, we certainly aught to be prophetic. We should *all* be seers in other words.

I fell at his feet to worship him. And he said unto me, See thou do it not: I am thy fellow servant, and of thy brethren that have the testimony of Jesus: worship God: **FOR THE TESTIMONY OF JESUS IS THE SPIRIT OF PROPHECY.**

(Revelation 19:10)

To that end, seers can SEE! They can see what the Spirit is doing and can also hear what the Spirit is saying *(to the Church)*. We are not mute spiritually speaking and must live out our lives with all five-senses functioning in both realms!

Do you have eyes but fail to see, and ears but fail to hear?

(Mark 8:18 NIV)

He who is able to hear, let him **LISTEN TO <u>AND</u> HEED WHAT THE [HOLY] SPIRIT SAYS** *to the assemblies (churches).*

(Revelation 2:7 AMPC)

The knowledge of the secrets of the kingdom of God has been given to you, but to others I speak in parables, so that, **though seeing, they may not see; though hearing, they may not understand.**

(Luke 8:10 NIV)

Their eyes are open but don't see a thing, Their ears are open but don't hear a thing.

(Vs. 10 MSG)

A Heavenly Perspective

We must see and hear prophetically *(from a heavenly perspective)*, as the Father sees things and stay open to that realm all the time *(living a three-dimensional life: spirit first, then soul and body).*

For me personally, I am always led by an inner witness and time alone praying. In many cases when it's hardest to hear God, it's because the circumstances are shouting so loudly.

Dictating and telling us to do things in a particular way, while at the same time *(inwardly)* there is a gentle and peaceful knowing: *"That's not how it is… this is the way you should go."* Sometimes this inner leading can go crosswise with logic and reason.

Now let me tell you, I am and always have been a big advocate for common sense, *(in other words using our heads is important too)* except whenever it's at the expense of being led by the Spirit of God!

The Bottom Line:

Are we willing to trust God in the unknown? Or in that, which has not fully been revealed to us yet? In most cases all that is required, is for us to take a step of faith.

It's true to say, He cannot lead you until you are honestly willing to obey Him. Being totally available to Him, whatever He wants to do in and through your life. The Holy Spirit is the Spirit of truth who convinces the world of sin, righteousness and judgment *(John 16:8).* He will show you exactly where you are spiritually; you will learn not to move a step further until you agree with Him.

Romans 8:14 says: those who are led by the Spirit of God are sons of God. God leads you to do the things, which you really want to do deep inside.

Someone once asked, *"This vision is too large for me, it's like trying to eat an elephant. How can anyone possibly eat an elephant?"* The answer came, *"Just one bite at a time!"* (I like it!)

Remember, the only way that we are going to walk prophetically is if we allow the Holy Spirit to minister to us. You could say that we have to develop our spiritual muscles. They must become stronger than our natural abilities or our natural muscles.

No Easy Formulas

We must live out of our spirit and not our flesh. Out of our relationship with the Lord. That's the most important thing and **there are no particular guidelines or easy formulas for:** *"this is how you do it."*

> *They're full of FORMULAS and programs and advice, PEDDLING TECHNIQUES for getting what you want from God. Don't fall for that nonsense.*
> (Matthew 6:10 MSG)

On the other hand, the Holy Spirit is always fresh and always revelational *(always revealing and unravelling truth)* and will *always* take us forward.

To live prophetically means depending on Him for guidance, direction and daily instruction *(for both realms and*

EAGLES OF DESTINY ...a Prophetic Concept

in both kingdoms). We are in this world but not of it. Yet we must succeed in both: "...on earth as in heaven" *(Matthew 6:10).* God manifests His will in both:

> *Bring about Your kingdom.* **MANIFEST YOUR WILL HERE ON EARTH, AS IT IS MANIFEST IN HEAVEN.**
>
> *(Matthew 6:10 VOICE)*

> *Seek (aim at and strive after)* <u>**FIRST**</u> **OF ALL HIS KINGDOM** *and His righteousness (His way of doing and being right)...*
>
> *(Matthew 6:33 AMPC)*

CHAPTER 4

Fresh Revelation

A Direct Download

Taking this prophetic concept to another level, as we look at eagles in connection with Christianity, I would say that mature believers should always live by faith, *(fresh)* revelation, directly from the mouth of God.

Man shall not live by bread alone, but by every word that proceedeth out of the mouth of God.

(Matthew 4:4)

For me this has always referred, not only to the Logos *(written letter)*, "the revealed will of God" or "the sum utterances of God," the "divine expression of God..." In fact when holding the Bible, we are literally holding the sum total of the combined sayings of God in our hands. Rhema on the other hand is "the singular saying of God."

As it suggests, direct revelation, is not in-direct revelation. It is not regurgitated, or passed on information but is part of an active relationship with God. Revelation is fresh from the source, a direct download. It represents the NOW WORD of God in our lives and keeps us healthy.

Thankfully we are not living in the time of the Old Testament without direct access to the throne of God. The veil of separation from the Holy of Holies in the temple was torn in two; symbolic of our unrestricted access through the sacrificial blood of Jesus Christ.

> *Having therefore, brethren, boldness to* **ENTER INTO THE HOLIEST BY THE BLOOD OF JESUS...**
> *(Hebrews 10:19)*

Living by Fresh Revelation

We can hear God's voice directly. We don't have to go through the prophets of Old or Catholic priests of today! Scripture tells us: *"He that hath an ear, let him hear what the Spirit saith unto the churches" (Revelation 3:22).* Although God was speaking very specifically to seven individual churches, in the book of Revelation; it doesn't alter the fact, that WE today are the "Church of The Living God." Not of bricks and mortar but lively stones:

> **YOU ALSO, LIKE <u>LIVING STONES</u>, ARE BEING BUILT INTO A SPIRITUAL HOUSE** *to be a holy*

priesthood, offering spiritual sacrifices acceptable to God through Jesus Christ.

(1 Peter 2:5-9 NIV)

Only intimate fellowship with the Holy Spirit can prevent us from backsliding, *"...hear what the **SPIRIT** saith," (Revelation 3:22),* and a living connection or relationship that regularly hears the voice of God.

All revelation that we receive will alter our lives forever. Those life-changing moments have the capacity to go on influencing and nourishing us for the rest of our lives.

For no man ever yet hated his own flesh; but **<u>NOURISHETH</u> AND CHERISHETH IT, EVEN AS THE LORD THE CHURCH.**

(Ephesians 5:29)

On the other hand, some revelation is like "daily bread," which is only good for the day we're in and no more. It quickly becomes stale and in the face of tomorrow's needs, grows quickly irrelevant. Does God's voice go stale? No! But in the wilderness, He kept the children of Israel reliant and dependent on Him for every single meal. The sea didn't part every day, but manna arrived everyday! We must grow accustomed to hearing God's voice every day.

Revelation Must be Gathered

It's great having those big moments in life, that change the course of history but they don't happen everyday. Usually in those big moments, we receive fresh direction and instruction that changes our course, but it's the daily manna that sustains us. It sustained the Israelites for 40 years! *(Incidentally God did not spoon-feed them, they had to apply themselves and gather the manner everyday. Revelation must be gathered).*

God did not make it easy for them. Even though He fed them, and their clothes did not grow old or wear out, they still had to depend on Him every day to sustain themselves. They were not allowed to hoard manna up. They had to be thrown on God everyday! Likewise we can't say, *"I went to church for a few weeks, that will keep me going for the rest of the year!"*

For example, if they tried to keep their manna for the next day it would rot and grow worms! Am I saying that yesterday's revelation is rotten? Not quite! Rhema never rots! Nevertheless, what applies today, doesn't automatically apply in our tomorrows.

And if we're trying to obey what God was saying a decade ago or even a year or a month ago, without any idea what He is saying today, we're going to miss it completely.

The result will be spiritual frustration! People who try going backwards to go forwards, usually end up going nowhere!

CHAPTER 5

Overcoming Spiritual Frustration

The Staircase to Nowhere

I knew of a dear Christian woman many years ago that used to have recurring dreams. Now these dreams weren't violent or sexual in nature, so they weren't nightmares filled with fear in that sense, but they were fuelled with frustration, spiritual confusion and despair.

She dreamt simply of being on an escalator *(electronic walking staircase)*, similar to those found in airports. In her dream it was always moving yet never arriving. It wasn't taking her anywhere.

She knew this reoccurring dream was representative of her life. Always exerting much energy, always working hard, always busy and sincere, but in danger of going nowhere. She would wake up feeling worn out, discouraged and confused.

There are a lot of people living like this. Wasting energy going nowhere, with intelligence that has no direction! In her dream she would eventually be running and sweating, desperately trying to out-run the escalator's speed, so that she could eventually arrive somewhere and get off... but there was never any sense of fulfilment. She was always left feeling exhausted and frustrated.

Another dream she would have, with a similar theme, was all about trying to get out of her house for some important pressing engagement. But in the dream she was never able to get out of the house.

Her shoes, her clothes, her make-up, her keys and so on, would always be mysteriously missing. She would frantically search to find these items and then something else would happen to prevent her leaving.

It was a dream with the feeling of panic, letting people down, shame and failure. Always racing towards everything at break-neck-speed with maximum effort but to no avail. Both dreams were filled with frustration and confusion. Eventually she got free of this torment but how many people suffer like this in real life?

Stupor and Spiritual Inertia

I also knew a young gentleman who strove for years to find his true niche in life. Once he found what he was good at, he won a generous scholarship at a very prestigious art school, and worked day and night filled with passion in his heart and thanking God. Then one day for no apparent reason, he just lost his motivation and a spirit of stupor came upon him.

He could no longer function. Even though he was passionate about achieving his dreams he could no longer stay focused or keep a grasp on his inspiration.

All the doors of divine favour and financial breakthroughs now seemed to mean nothing. Just when it all seemed like his dreams where coming true, distractions came and swallowed up his creativeness and motivation. What was happening?

There are several possible reasons for this. The first could be sabotage, plain old spiritual warfare. The devil will not take our success lying down. If the last few pages have been speaking to you, then let me suggest my book on "Healing and Deliverance," you will find it an interesting read, which will help one understand Satan's network of operations. Other subjects in question: Can a Christian be Demonised or Oppressed; The Effects of the Occult etc.[4]

Pray and Declare

"Lord, you lift up those who are bowed down. Therefore, I am strong and my heart takes courage. I establish myself on righteousness – right standing in conformity with Your will and order. I am far even from the thought of oppression or destruction, for I fear not. I am far from terror, for it shall not come near me.

Father, You have thoughts and plans for my welfare and my peace. My mind is stayed on You, for I stop allowing myself to be agitated and disturbed and intimidated and cowardly unsettled."

"Satan, I resist you and every oppressive spirit in the name of Jesus. I resist fear, discouragement, self-pity, and depression. I speak the Word of truth, in the power of God, and I give you no place, Satan; I give no opportunity to you. **I am delivered** *from oppression* **by the blood of the Lamb."**[5]

It's our duty to plead the blood of Jesus and to bind the devil *(see Revelation 12:11; James 4:7; Matthew 16:19; 18:18-19).*

A Picture of Diligent Endurance

Praise God, we can be set free, the chains are broken, but those dreams seemed so real, they were filled with frustration and confusion, because the source of our original inspiration was not valid in the first place! You can't sustain what was not truly yours.

Finally, there is such a thing, as an undisciplined mind. **Many great talents have been wasted and lost forever because people simply did not cultivate any discipline in their lives.**

It's important that we are not poor finishers. We must see things through and not just run with them for a while and then quit. We need to surrender our lives back to the Lord. Allow Him to take the lead once again, by humbling ourselves. Then the Holy Spirit will help us, not only to stand our ground but to *keep* our ground too!

*Therefore put on God's complete armour, that you may be able to resist **and STAND YOUR GROUND** on the evil day [of danger], and, **HAVING DONE ALL [THE CRISIS DEMANDS], TO STAND [FIRMLY IN YOUR PLACE]**.*

(Ephesians 6:13 AMPC)

Just Keep Standing

In the Wycliffe Bible, it simply says, *"... **in all things stand perfect**."* Creating a picture of diligent endurance, of doing what we know to be right and just keeping on, keeping on!

For instance when we get to the other side of a crisis, and we no longer know what to do, we must just keep doing what God showed us to do before.

Jesus said that we would always have troubles *(see John 16:33)*. One crisis after another will come our way as long as we live, regardless of how well insulated we try to make ourselves.

Myles Munroe in his book "Overcoming Crisis, the Secrets to Thriving in Challenging Times" says: "It is important to get a grip on how to overcome not only some of the circumstances, but also *(especially)* our emotional responses to difficulties. If we can regain our emotional footing in a storm, we will be able to overcome. First, before we can regain our emotional footing, we need to put our feet on the Rock-solid foundation of God."[6]

However if we are more adjusted to handle the struggles and failures of this life, rather than success, *(because we understand the battle better),* **then what happens when we win?**

For some of us, we don't know how to handle success because we fear the weight of expectation attached to it.

The fact is, we should just keep doing what God already showed us in the beginning and just keep **STANDING OUR GROUND and SPEAKING WHAT GOD SAYS!**

CHAPTER 6

Spiritual Energy

His Flight Pattern is Strategic

Howeover, if people spend all their spiritual energy getting from A to B, they will be depleted *(defeated)* when they arrive. They push through many obstacles to get where they need to be and then collapse *(backslide)*.

Eagles are careful not to use up all their energy reserves. That's why they rest in their vantage point. Even their flight pattern is strategic, in order to conserve energy. To lose too much energy is death for an eagle. He has to balance his hunting, eating, resting etc., so that he does not become depleted.

Even in the military, soldiers get leave. They come off the front lines to recoup and visit home. We can't always be in battle. There is reprieve. There is a place of rest. In Christ whose yoke is easy and burden is light.

Are you tired? Worn out? Burned out on religion? Come to me. **GET AWAY WITH ME AND YOU'LL RECOVER YOUR LIFE. I'LL SHOW YOU HOW TO TAKE A REAL REST.**

Walk with me and work with me – watch how I do it. **LEARN THE UNFORCED RHYTHMS OF GRACE.** *I won't lay anything heavy or ill-fitting on you.* **KEEP COMPANY WITH ME AND YOU'LL LEARN TO LIVE FREELY AND LIGHTLY.**

(Matthew 11:30 MSG)

With Overcoming Poise

On the other hand we must always be suited in readiness with our spiritual armour, even when there is no battle raging. Getting the balance right between conserving spiritual energy *(opposed to burning-out)* and living ready and prepared. This is something we can learn from the eagle that is always rested, but also always learning his environment, his prey, his competition *(adversary)* and his surroundings – by stealth and surveillance.

We too must not be *"ignorant of Satan's devices,"* even when there is no battle going on. We must remain in a position of being watchful and alert.

One ploy of our enemy is to encourage us to wear-ourselves-out so that we are no threat to him. **An exhausted eagle is a poor hunter.** His faculties and senses are off. His accuracy is impaired. **Equally for us, RESTING in Christ (*in heavenly places*) must be our highest priority.**

Only then can we remain ready to swoop down from a position of strength, authority and victory, into situations that normally have overwhelmed us, if we had not been getting our strength, strategy and inspiration from above.

All other inspiration will wane and wax cold. It will run out of steam. When we depend on it most, it will fail us. Writers get writers block, artists lose their creativeness, workers lose incentive, students lose motivation, athletes lose impetus and designers lose inspiration and lovers lose their passion! There's a lot to lose.

Stepped into Reasoning

Reinhard Bonnke once said, *"My flame has never gone out."* Meaning that the anointing he originally received had never grown old and that he had no need for some *"new anointing!"*

I would further that by saying, when we step into burn-out-mode it's usually because we've stepped into reasoning. Then automatically the development of stress steps in! Only the anointing can sustain us and carry us within our lives. **It's the anointing that breaks the yoke of bondage.**

It shall come to pass in that day, that his burden shall be taken away from off thy shoulder, and his yoke from off thy neck, and THE YOKE SHALL BE DESTROYED BECAUSE OF THE ANOINTING.

(Isaiah 10:27)

It shall be in that day, his burden shall be taken away from thy shoulder, and his yoke from thy neck; and **THE YOKE SHALL WAX [ALL] ROTTEN FROM THE FACE OF OIL...** *the yoke shall be destroyed because of the anointing.*

(Isaiah 10:27 WYC)

Protection and Boldness

In addition to this, Paul prayed for two things, protection and boldness. FIRE TO FULFIL THE CALL. *"That I may declare it boldly and courageously, as I ought to do."*

PROTECTION:
Finally, brethren, pray for us, that the word of the Lord may have free course, and be glorified, even as it is with you:

And that we may be **DELIVERED FROM UNREASONABLE AND WICKED MEN:** *for all men have not faith.*

(2 Thessalonians 3:1-4)

BOLDNESS:
Praying always... and for me, that utterance may be given unto me, **THAT I MAY OPEN MY MOUTH BOLDLY,** *to make known the mystery of the gospel, for which I am an ambassador in bonds:* **THAT THEREIN I MAY SPEAK BOLDLY, AS I OUGHT TO SPEAK.**

(Ephesians 6:18-20)

CHAPTER 7

Our Overcoming Position in Christ

Position is Possession

What dose it mean to overcome in life? To overcome is to prevail over the circumstances by remaining seated with Christ *(in the heavenly places)*. Position is everything. Only by keeping our position in Christ can we see things from His perspective:

He that OVERCOMETH shall inherit ALL THINGS...

(Revelation 21:7)

TO KEEP SATAN FROM GETTING THE ADVANTAGE OVER US; FOR WE ARE NOT IGNORANT OF HIS WILES AND INTENTIONS.

(2 Corinthians 2:11 AMPC)

It is important to stress without overstating, that like the eagle, we must ALWAYS come from a position that is above and not beneath, a position of success, strength and victory (*not defeat*) - in Christ Jesus.

> *If ye then be risen with Christ,* **SEEK THOSE THINGS WHICH ARE ABOVE,** *where Christ sitteth on the right hand of God.*
>
> (*Colossians 3:1*)

> *So if you're serious about living this new resurrection life with Christ,* **act** *like it. Pursue the things over which Christ presides.*

> *Don't shuffle along, eyes to the ground, absorbed with the things right in front of you.* **LOOK UP, AND BE ALERT** *to what is going on around Christ — that's where the action is.* **SEE THINGS FROM HIS PERSPECTIVE.**
>
> (*Colossians 3:1 MSG*)

Spiritual Vantage Point

This is where we have to learn cool, poised composure like the eagle. He does not fret or flap around in panic. His great wings are not made for frantic flight but for gliding. That's why he makes his home in the heights of the trees or the mountain crags. So that he can take to the air with ease. It's much harder for the eagle to get airborne from level ground, than it is from an elevated position.

His great wingspan means that he requires much room (*without obstruction*) to open those imposing wings. Getting airborne from the ground also requires much more energy than being caught up in the updrafts from his vantage point.

Our vantage point is Christ. Interestingly the winds are greater in the heights. Where the currents are. That's where believers ought to be. There is no anointing to lift us, *(to be caught up in)* if we are grovelling around on the floor like turkeys or chickens.

DON'T SHUFFLE ALONG, EYES TO THE GROUND, absorbed with the things right in front of you. LOOK UP... TO WHAT IS GOING ON AROUND CHRIST — THAT'S WHERE THE ACTION IS.
(Colossians 3:1 MSG)

Likewise when we get grounded with our faith, it's a lot harder to get back up again. We must stay in the heights. Even when an eagle swoops to catch its prey, it won't stay down for very long. It's too dangerous.

Timing is part of the eagle's overall strategy. He has no business *(and no comfort)* being grounded for too long.

Your Resting - His Advantage

We must see the lesson in this. An eagle will spend as little time on the ground as possible. That doesn't mean he flies none stop. But he will perch high in the trees or mountain crags. Always at his vantage point! *(His resting point is also his vantage point).*

We too have a spiritual vantage point and we must stay there, and be overcoming as God intended. That's what it means to be seated with Christ in heavenly places!

*And hath raised us up together, and made us **SIT TOGETHER IN HEAVENLY PLACES** in Christ Jesus.*

(Ephesians 2:6)

*And did raise [us] up together, and **DID SEAT [US] TOGETHER IN THE HEAVENLY [PLACES] IN CHRIST JESUS.***

(YLT)

Notice that there are seated positions and standing positions spiritually speaking. One scripture tells us to STAND and the other scripture tells us that we are to be SEATED with Christ!

Only in the heavenly realms we can sit! The eagle will never sit on the ground. But it will sit in his vantage point for many hours. Likewise we must recognise where our vantage point is *(and where it is not)*. Our vantage point is in Christ alone. Only in Him can we afford to sit watching like the eagle does.

Nevertheless there will be times when we must swoop to the earth, but must never lose sight of where our true position lies: *"Be not conformed to this world" (Romans 12:2); "They are not of the world, even as I am not of the world" (John 17:16).*

Don't Grow Battle Weary

Believers who are battle weary or have lost sight of where their true position, must get back to their place with Christ in the heavenly realms.

Soldiers, who never take leave, grow weary in battle. God the Father does not want all of His children to be battle weary. He has provided us relief in Christ.

*LET US NOT LOSE HEART AND GROW WEARY AND FAINT... for in due time **and** at the appointed season we shall reap, if we do not loosen **and** relax our courage **and** faint.*
(Galatians 6:9 AMPC)

*For My yoke is wholesome (useful, good — not harsh, hard, sharp, or pressing, but comfortable, gracious, and pleasant), and My burden is light **and** easy to be borne.*
(Matthew 11:30 AMPC)

So for all those who are still asking, "How do we overcome?" The answer is simple: "We overcome in Christ alone." Our eyes must always be fixed on Him and our position must be seated with Him in heavenly places.

He makes the difference in our lives and there's no alternative or a substitute. **Humanity has always tried to be its own saviour.**

But for all **those who depend on Christ, overcoming is preordained, unavoidable and inevitable!**

CHAPTER 8

All Consuming Life!

Let the Word be Pure

It has been suggested by many that eagles don't eat dead meat. However this is not entirely true. Their natural first choice and preference is fresh prey, captured alive, still raw and fresh. But they will eat dead animals too! To stay alive, healthy and strong the eagle must eat well.

However not all eagles are created equal, and not all eagles behave the same, but generally eagles prefer fresh food but will take advantage of carrion too.

Perhaps I could suggest that when eagles do eat other dead animals *(carrion - dead and putrefying flesh)* it's possibly an indication that fresh food is in shorter supply. As stated an eagle thrives best on fresh meat. We prefer to think of the vulture as a scavenger and the eagle as the majestic hunter, but the fact of the matter is, the eagle will scavenge too!

While the "Bald Eagle" might be the national symbol for the US and perceived as regal and all-powerful, don't be fooled by this magnificent creature because the eagle is no saint *(we can characterise this as fallen nature)* of noble character! It can be a thieving imposter too!

Just because it likes its meat raw and fresh, does not mean that his captures are always honest gain. The Bald Eagle especially, can be a bit of a pirate and has no qualms about seizing the fresh meat from another hunter's hard earned spoils.

A Fresh Word is Always Best

"BALD EAGLES PREFER FRESH FOOD, BUT WILL ALSO EAT CARRION OR STEAL FROM OTHER PREDATORS. A dead deer or seal is a feast for Bald Eagles, but dead fish along the shore are also choice pickings. Some Bald Eagles even steal fish from another large fishing bird, the Osprey, in midair!"[7]

In fact Benjamin Franklin, one of the Founding Fathers of the USA, was not easily seduced by the Bald Eagle's grandiose image and gave a scathing character assessment for it, *(as seen in both sources below)* in objection and firm opposition to it being used as the national symbol; preferring instead the native turkey:

"In 1782, when the Second Continental Congress was considering the Bald Eagle as the symbol of the newly formed United States, Benjamin Franklin was not very supportive of the idea. **He wrote to his daughter of his disapproval of the choice because THE BALD EAGLE HAD A 'BAD MORAL CHARACTER.'**

He believed that the eagle was lazy because it stole food from hawks. He also felt it was easily frightened by smaller birds (*source: Franklin Institute*). Instead, Franklin wanted the turkey to be the fledgling nation's symbol."

(*Parable: Remember the turkey has the form of religion but has no power*).

"While he thought the turkey was slightly 'vain and silly,' he believed that the turkey displayed its courage by hunting for its own food."[8]

The following is an excerpt from the letter to Franklin's daughter:

"For my own part I wish the Bald Eagle had not been chosen the Representative of our Country. HE IS A BIRD OF BAD MORAL CHARACTER. HE DOES NOT GET HIS LIVING HONESTLY. You may have seen him perched on some dead tree near the river, where, too lazy to fish for himself, he watches the labour of the Fishing Hawk; and when that diligent bird has at length taken a fish, and is bearing it to his nest for the support of his mate and young ones, the Bald Eagle **pursues him and takes it from him.**

WITH ALL THIS INJUSTICE, HE IS NEVER IN GOOD CASE BUT LIKE THOSE AMONG MEN WHO LIVE BY SHARPING & ROBBING HE IS GENERALLY POOR AND OFTEN VERY LOUSY.

BESIDES HE IS A RANK COWARD: The little King Bird, not bigger than a Sparrow, attacks him boldly and drives him out of the district. He is therefore by no means a proper emblem for the brave and honest…

I am on this account not displeased that the figure is not known as a Bald Eagle, but looks more like a Turkey. For the truth the Turkey is in comparison a much more respectable bird, and withal a true original Native of America...”

(Religion is always more respected than those Born again spirit field eagle folk).

“HE IS BESIDES, THOUGH A LITTLE VAIN & SILLY, A BIRD OF COURAGE, and would not hesitate to attack a grenadier of the British Guards who should presume to invade his farm yard with a red coat on.”[9]

Interestingly things can be seen from a *very* different perspective. For example the turkey is not a meat eater, therefore could never be seen as a valiant predator *(hunter/ killer!)* President John F. Kennedy later wrote:

“The Founding Fathers made an appropriate choice when they selected the Bald Eagle as the emblem of the nation. **THE FIERCE BEAUTY AND PROUD INDEPENDENCE** of this great bird aptly symbolizes the strength and freedom of America.”[10]

*He that waits upon the Lord shall renew their strength
(and freedom); they shall mount up with wings as eagles...
(Isaiah 40:31, emphasis added)*

Things could have look quite different had it been a turkey!

Picture Reference[11]

CHAPTER 9

The Fallen Nature Reverts

The Dark Side

Perhaps the eagle's dark side is not something that we want to parallel with, except its penchant for fresh meat! Eagles do eat carrion but its staple is fresh fish.

We could say that an eagle that reverts to its fallen nature will steal or eat dead meat. And a thriving eagle *(spiritually speaking)*, full of life and health has no need for dead meat and will choose fresh meat every time *(the healthier the meat, the healthier the bird)*. We know for instance that our fallen nature will always try and revert to its old ways:

*Like a dog who goes back to his own vomit, so is **A FOOL WHO ALWAYS RETURNS TO HIS FOOLISHNESS.***
(Proverbs 26:11 VOICE)

*Of them the proverbs are true: "**A dog returns to its vomit**," and, "**A sow that is washed returns to her wallowing in the mud.**"*

(2 Peter 2:22 NIV)

Dead Letter is Always Religion

Likewise Christians under pressure will look to satisfy themselves instead of pushing into the Rhema *(fresh meat of God's Word i.e. Revelation!)* Instead we try to feed ourselves with dead letter and religion; then fail to thrive!

When fresh meat *(rhema/revelation)* is available and in abundant supply, why settle for spiritual carrion *(dead letter)?* **It's just laziness that reaches for the dead instead of the living!** It might take more effort, but is less toxic!

Eagles love fish and living not far from water ensures an abundant supply.

*The Lord governeth me, and there is nothing that I shall lack... in the place of pasture there he hath set me. **HE NOURISHED ME ON THE WATER OF REFRESHING.***

(Psalm 23:1-2 WYC)

Scavengers will eat anything, even if it's toxic road-kill with the stench of death:

"It's said, Vultures are carnivorous and eat carrion almost exclusively. **They... are able to consume carcasses that may have rotted so much as to be dangerous for other animals.** This gives vultures a unique and important ecological niche because they help prevent the spread of diseases from old, rotting corpses."[12]

We must not be spiritual scavengers and settle with anything. We must not be found eating carrion *(prophetically speaking!)* Prophets must push through to the third heaven *(the Holy of Holies)* where the throne room of God is and where the revelation is clear, holy, pure and unadulterated *(without mixture)*.

Spiritual Filtering

God has given us the ability of discernment, to distinguish between good and evil, life and death. If we are not dull! We have the ability therefore to filter.

If taken literally, we too must filter *(to the best of our ability)* all incoming daily downloads *(spiritually speaking)*. There's no question that a Christian must choose LIFE and be responsible for what they consume on a daily basis and be selective.

Downloads can include what we take in through our: eyes, ears, mouths or even sexually. There are many entry points into our lives, so we must be vigilant.[13]

> *I call heaven and earth to record this day against you, that I have set before you life and death, blessing and cursing:* **THEREFORE CHOOSE LIFE,** *that both thou and thy seed may live.*
>
> *(Deuteronomy 30:19)*

If healthy eagles that have access to an abundant food supply will instinctively choose fresh prey over something dead, *(sick, old and rotting)*, we too must instinctively discern the living from the dead.

What type of language, music, films, books or company we allow to influence our lives is crucial!

Do not be so deceived and misled! Evil companionships (communion, associations) corrupt and deprave good manners and morals and character.
(1 Corinthians 15:33 AMPC)

Filtered by the Crop

"Bald eagles do not have to eat every day, but if the bird goes too long without food, it may not be able to hunt effectively enough to survive.

Eagles have an out pouching of the oesophagus, called a crop, where they can store food when the stomach is full.

THE CROP ALSO SEPARATES INDIGESTIBLE SUBSTANCES, SUCH AS FEATHERS, FUR, AND SCALES FROM THE MEAT. The indigestible substance is mixed with mucus and formed into a mass. After the meal, **THE EAGLE EVENTUALLY REGURGITATES THE MASS AS A CASTING."**[14]

For me the crop acts like a naturally built in filtering system. Not all birds have crops but many do. *(A crop is an expanded, muscular pouch near the gullet or throat)*. However birds of prey, specifically eagles can become diseased if this indigestible matter is not dispelled properly *(creates blockage)*.

As I have already said, eagles lose energy very easily and must eat regularly to be healthy and to hunt well. **A BLOCKAGE CAN PUT AN EAGLE OUT OF ACTION.** In fact he cannot hunt or eat again until this blockage has been removed.

"Raptors in the wild generally eat whole carcass meals *(i.e. fur/feather, meat, bone and prey gut contents)* once daily. The indigestible fur and feather is referred to as 'casting' and is regurgitated as a 'casting or pellet' 12-18 hours after feeding.

One should never feed a bird again before it has cast its pellet, for fear of the subsequent meal forcing the casting into the small intestine and resulting in a blockage.

…As soon as the crop *(food storage organ on the front of the bird's neck)* is emptied, the bird can be fed again without any risk of blockage."[15]

CHAPTER 10

Toxins on the Rock

Bang out the Indigestible

It has been said, that when an eagle is having trouble expelling this mass of indigestible matter, he has been known to bang his beak on a rock to help dislodge it.

This creates a most wonderful analogy for the Christian believer. Because where better to bang out the toxins of our lives, than upon the ROCK OF AGES JESUS CHRIST!

King David poured out his complaint before the Lord, in his famous Psalms. We must not only filter the spiritually indigestible matter that is unavoidably part of our everyday existence, but we must not fail to expel it.

Going to God's Word brings freedom and keeps us free.

YE SHALL KNOW THE TRUTH, AND THE TRUTH
SHALL MAKE YOU FREE.

(John 8:32)

The trouble with this is that most people do suppress the junk in their lives and never actually get free of it. They take in more and more junk, on top of this, which just compounds the issue.

Then people wonder why they are not mounting up on wings like eagles and soaring in the Spirit. An eagle is only as healthy as his last meal. He must keep his energy up otherwise he cannot hunt and if he cannot hunt he cannot eat. This is like our relationship with the Word of God and revelation. It must be alive in us:

LET THE WORD [SPOKEN BY] CHRIST (THE
MESSIAH) HAVE ITS HOME [IN YOUR HEARTS
AND MINDS] AND **DWELL IN YOU IN [ALL ITS]**
RICHNESS, *as you teach and admonish* **and** *train one*
another in all insight **and** *intelligence* **and** *wisdom [in*
spiritual things, and as you sing] psalms and hymns and
spiritual songs, making melody to God with [His] grace
in your hearts.

(Colossians 3:16 AMPC)

If you abide in Me and My voice abides in you, anything
you ask will come to pass for you.

(John 15:7 VOICE)

Save Your Energy

This reminds me of the lion. He does not roar 24 hours a day nor does he spend his energy. In fact he probably sleeps

Toxins on the Rock

23 out of every 24 hours. The lionesses do the hunting and the lions go in for the final kill. They like the eagles conserve as much energy as possible. Even when an eagle flies, it is not using very much energy at all. It masters the wind, the currents and the updrafts and glides.

As believers our spiritual energy is very important and we must protect it like the Lion and the Eagle. Who are not frantic but are very precise. For them it is all about precision and strategy.

This is not to say we can be spiritually lazy. No. An eagle spends much of its time looking, perceiving, watching, knowing and learning *(its prey, territory etc)*. Its time conserving energy is not wasted, by no means. He is using his time well. Preparing.

Running around like a chicken with no head is not the "modus operandi" *(Latin: method of operation)* for the eagle. He is cool, collected and ready. We too must always be waiting on the Spirit. Knowing His next move. Where He wants us to be. What He wants us to do and to say. As we see here:

A heavenly messenger brought this **short** *message from the Lord to Philip* **during his time preaching in Samaria** *... Leave Samaria.* **Go south to the Jerusalem-Gaza road.**

The message was especially unusual because *this road runs through the middle of uninhabited desert.* **But Philip got up,** <u>**left the excitement of Samaria,**</u> **and did as he was told to do.**

Along this road, Philip saw a chariot in the distance. In the chariot was a dignitary from Ethiopia (the treasurer for Queen Candace), an African man who had been castrated. He had gone north to Jerusalem to worship at the Jewish temple, and he was now heading southwest on his way home.

He was seated in the chariot and was reading aloud from a scroll of the prophet Isaiah. **PHILIP RECEIVED ANOTHER PROMPTING FROM THE HOLY SPIRIT: Go over to the chariot and climb on board.**

(Acts 8:26-30 VOICE)

CHAPTER 11

The Now Word of God

His Voice is all the Provision You Need

Maturity *(or the hungry)* **always seeks out the NOW Word of God on a daily basis.** Hearing God's voice everyday will prevent us from wasting our energy on what does not bear any fruit. Will also break the chains of frustration in our lives and help us to move forwards in victory and without confusion.

We must apply ourselves to pursuing His heart every single day, by praying: "What is on Your heart today Lord?" "How can I apply Your will today - in the midst of this particular situation – on earth as it is in heaven?"

"Reveal Your will to me Lord. What is Your desire about this?" "Help me to understand what is happening right now, and give me the courage to follow Your instructions." "Your voice is my provision. Speak to me." He is always waiting for us!

The late Oral Roberts once said, "So we need to wait on God more *(expecting, looking and longing for Him),* by speaking and signing to Him more in tongues; communicating mysteries to God while building ourselves up in the Spirit and in faith at the same time.

It is times like this when we get so caught up in the spirit, that we can get visions and words from God. When praying in this way, we should seek the interpretation of what we are saying."[16]

THE NOW WORD OF GOD is what we should be seeking on a daily basis as eagles. In fact we have no business wasting our time pursuing anything else! This is what the mature spiritual eagle is seeking out.

He is in constant pursuit of his next meal, to avoid growing unnecessarily tired and weak. In other words he avoids pointless other activity and keeps his strength going. **WE ARE RESPONSIBLE FOR OUR OWN SPIRITUAL GROWTH OR DECLINE.**

Those who find Daily Nourishment, Thrive

We quickly lose the nourishment and strength of yesterday's bread. WE MUST FEED OUR SOULS DAILY upon the manna God has given us.

(Charles H. Spurgeon)[17]

Maturity involves responsibility. The eagle knows that without nourishment he will grow weak. He does not wait to be fed. He seeks and he finds what strengthens him.

"This is why you often see eagles soaring through the air. They are not merely out for a fun flight but are instead looking for food. Even though they don't have to eat every single day, it is important... as THEY CAN BECOME VERY TIRED AND WEAK VERY QUICKLY.

If this happens it makes it more difficult to find food later, so a constant search for food is the way they ensure there is always enough..."[18]

When we stop hearing God it is either because of sin, or because we have walked away *(backslidden)*. **RITUAL IS NOT A RELATIONSHIP AND GOING THROUGH THE MOTIONS IS RELIGIOUS. WE NEED TO HEAR FROM GOD PERSONALLY DAILY!**

Daily Supply Guarantees Freshness

We know from scripture that **"Every morning** the people went out and gathered it *(manna)*... By the time the sun became hot, **it had melted away"** *(Exodus 16:21 VOICE)*. Therefore manna was fresh every morning – but if left, soon melted away. It did not keep without spoiling.

Give us this day our **DAILY BREAD.**

(Matthew 6:11)

We only spoil revelation when we ignore it. When we don't listen or **write it down.** That's why I write books! God speaks EVERYDAY and that's why Jesus taught his disciples to pray: "Give us this day our daily bread."

> *Listen obediently to God ...nothing halfhearted here; you must return to God, your God, totally, heart and soul, holding nothing back...* **THE WORD IS RIGHT HERE AND NOW—AS NEAR AS THE TONGUE IN YOUR MOUTH, AS NEAR AS THE HEART IN YOUR CHEST. JUST DO IT!**
> *(Deuteronomy 30:10-14 MSG)*

God doesn't just speak once into our lives. We are meant to KEEP seeking and receiving from God. Consistency matters to God and He teaches us continuity by keeping back tomorrow's manna for tomorrow, so that we remain in a place of need and keep seeking Him.

In Christ everything has become new. We don't need to stick with the stale and the old. And we must not be deterred from our mission, from getting before God on a daily basis. The mature spiritual eagle is not easily deterred. He is always looking for something new and fresh.

> *The Lord's mercy and loving-kindness...they are* **NEW EVERY MORNING.**
> *(Lamentations 3:22-23 AMPC)*

> **OLD THINGS ARE PASSED AWAY; BEHOLD, ALL THINGS ARE BECOME NEW.**
> *(2 Corinthians 5:17)*

Our relationship with God is not to be defined by *yearly-pop-calls-and-visits* to His throne, but by our daily devotion, intimate and regular fellowship with Him. Often times we feel stale, because we have allowed the cares of this life to suck us dry and to rob us of this vital energy and joy fuelling discipline, called PRAYER.

Calendar Serving

I don't know about you, but I NEVER wanted to become just another Calendar-Serving-Christian, who along with the rest of society barley acknowledges God, except for religious holidays and rare family occasions *(such as Christmas, Easter, christenings, weddings or even funerals!)*

So, it's inevitable, that when we don't keep our relationship with God fresh and thriving, things in our lives will only begin to show signs of decay:

DON'T TRY TO KEEP ANY OF IT UNTIL THE MORNING. Either eat it all, or throw it away. But some people ignored Moses and tried to keep some of it until the next morning.

Overnight it became wormy and started to have a dreadful smell. Moses became furious with them because they had disobeyed God's instructions.
(Exodus 16:19-20 VOICE)

It was tough for the Israelites to learn this lesson perhaps? That without any guarantee for the next day's supply, they had to go to sleep at night, knowing there was zero food in their tents, for the next morning's breakfast! They had to believe that God - would do it again - and supernaturally provide.

In this way, God kept His people thrown upon Him. Keeping them in a position of trusting Him DAILY.

CHAPTER 12

Craving Onions

Those who Complain Remain

I wonder how we would have felt, had we eaten the same thing and worn the same clothes for 40 years! Hard to imagine perhaps, but maybe we would have complained much more than the children of Israel did! After all they did not have much by way of creature comforts surrounding them there in the wilderness.

I wager, that our flesh is no different today than theirs was then. Our flesh is addicted to comfort and fulfilling its appetites. Even if we had feared joining the bickering and debate, we most certainly would have joined the thought process! It's hard going without, after you have been used to plenty.

On the human measure of things, let's just remember that they were not surrounded by any modern technology *(including flushing toilets!)* Equally there were no fast food restaurants, just the same thing to eat every day. There was no variety of taste or change of scene.

So there's little wonder they grew weary and started craving the cucumbers and melons, leeks, onions, and garlic of their captivity *(Egypt!)* Notice they didn't crave any hardship, just what their appetites were dictating.

Appetites Wage War!

Incidentally notice how it was for the Egyptians *(who had escaped with them)*; they were also longing, "for the good things of Egypt." It's called wanting the best of both worlds. How quick the flesh forgets! How quickly the appetites wage war!

Then the Egyptians who had come with them began to long for the good things of Egypt. *This added to the discontent of the people of Israel and they wept, "Oh, for a few bites of meat!*

Oh, that we had some of the delicious fish we enjoyed so much in Egypt, and the wonderful cucumbers and melons, leeks, onions, and garlic!"

(Numbers 11:5 TLB)

"Oh, that we were back in Egypt," they moaned, "and that the Lord had killed us there! For there we had plenty to eat. But now you have brought us into this wilderness to kill us with starvation."

(Exodus 16:3 TLB)

I have always preached the same message where this is concerned. **YOU CAN GET THE PEOPLE OUT OF EGYPT BUT NOT ALWAYS EGYPT OUT OF THE PEOPLE!**

Accomplish the Mission

The same applies; you can get the people out of the world, but not always the world out of the people. I'll say it again; it takes a stern commitment, like that of the eagle *(to stay the course)* who **locks focus to accomplish his mission.**

God is never obliged to furnish our wants and selfish appetites, but to meet our genuine needs. That's what He did in that wilderness and all they were required to do was to trust God every single day of their lives without complaining. **Complaining about the journey or the provision is the Christian's downfall!** Those who complain remain.

For the kingdom of God is not meat and drink; but righteousness, and peace, and joy in the Holy Ghost.

(Romans 14:17)

As it's important to have a conscious knowledge of what the Kingdom of God is, I will give you two other very good versions of the same verse:

The kingdom of God is not a matter of [getting the] food and drink [one likes], *but instead it is righteousness (that state which makes a person acceptable to God) and [heart] peace and joy in the Holy Spirit.*

(Romans 14:17 AMPC)

The kingdom of God is not about eating and drinking.
When God reigns, the order of the day is redeeming justice,
true peace, and joy made possible by the Holy Spirit.
(VOICE)

Millennials or Generation "Y"

Let me ask a pointed question: "What out of all your creature comforts and hi-Tec possessions – would you find hardest to give up for one entire day?"

Particularly for the younger folks, it would be their smart-phone or high-speed Internet connection! My guess is that *most* people would find this equally difficult. Many of us have not just grown accustomed but dependent on such things!

But it's easy to forget that young people today have never experienced or known life without such amenities.

"Generation Y covers people born between the 1980's and the year 2000, and these individuals are sometimes referred to as Gen Y, the Millennial Generation, or simply Millennials.

GENERATION Y HAS BEEN SHAPED BY THE TECHNOLOGICAL REVOLUTION that occurred throughout their youth. **GEN Y GREW UP WITH TECHNOLOGY, SO BEING CONNECTED AND TECH SAVVY IS IN THEIR DNA.**

Equipped with latest technology and gadgets, such as iPhones, laptops and lately tablets, **GENERATION Y IS ONLINE AND CONNECTED 24/7, 365 DAYS A YEAR.**

Many Millennials grew up seeing their Baby Boomer parents working day and night doing stressful corporate jobs, which has shaped their own views on the workforce and the need for work-life balance."[19]

Family Fast - so God Comes First

This is where fasting comes in *(for our family at least!)* Fasting is still relevant today. It deals with the appetites. It helps us to make a conscious decision to put our flesh in an uncomfortable position for a while! To let the appetites know that they are not in charge – and you've decided to live to focus only on what God wants instead *(see Isaiah 1:19)*.

My family and I fast every Sunday, but its not food that we fast, but technology! We dedicate the entire day to God. So there can be no TV, radio, laptops, smart-devices of any kind, *(only Christian music, prayer and bible reading is allowed for one whole day in every week)*. It was difficult at first.

There were complaints. But we have come to enjoy it and look forward to it. In fact it has become a very special day for our family. We have also noticed, that as we give ourselves deeper to God *(without any outside distractions)* we actually bond closer as a family in the process. Such a decision has helped my family bear *"peaceable fruits of righteousness"* and I urge you to do the same!

For the time being no discipline brings joy, but seems grievous and painful; but afterwards ***IT YIELDS A PEACEABLE FRUIT OF RIGHTEOUSNESS TO THOSE WHO HAVE BEEN TRAINED BY IT** [a*

harvest of fruit which consists in righteousness – in conformity to God's will in purpose, thought, and action, resulting in right living and right standing with God].
                                                    (Hebrews 12:11 AMPC)

*At the time, discipline isn't much fun. It always feels like it's going against the grain. Later, of course, **IT PAYS OFF HANDSOMELY, FOR IT'S THE WELL-TRAINED WHO FIND THEMSELVES MATURE IN THEIR RELATIONSHIP WITH GOD.***
                                                    (Hebrews 12:11 MSG)

CHAPTER 13

Riding the Thermals

Brilliant Aerodynamics

While it has never been proven that eagles love the storm, it is true however, that they soar and use the air currents. It is possible that during a storm they could use the wind to lift them.

But it is a stretch, without any real factual or scientific proof, to claim that the eagle loves the storm or even flies above it - yet the blogosphere is awash with teaching on this very subject.

Without doubt eagles are aerodynamically sound and subject to God's brilliance and design! The eagle instinctively understands the great thermals and updrafts; provided for it by nature and uses them to his advantage!

But you, beloved, build yourselves up [founded] on your most holy faith [MAKE PROGRESS, RISE LIKE AN EDIFICE HIGHER AND HIGHER], praying in the Holy Spirit.

(Jude 1:20 AMPC)

Likewise we need to use the wind of God's Spirit to make us rise higher and higher in life, by faith possessing airspace for God's Kingdom!

Eagles glide to rest their wings. They know how to ride the wind and let it lift them. They don't fight the wind. They go with it like the great currents out at sea. We also can regain our strength as we rest on the thermals of God's Spirit. Inhaling and gliding - taking in all that God has for us.

Eagles and Storms

I read some information that stated eagles fly into storms, use the winds of the storm to gain altitude, and that they rise way above the storm.

Peter Nye, from New York "Department of Environmental Conservation" said, "I have never heard of this behaviour exactly as you describe it. This sounds like stretching or misinterpreting what eagles do. Eagles definitely do use the winds *(and some quite strong)*, as well as 'updrafts' coming off hills and mountains.

This helps them to gain altitude and set them up for a long, soaring flight to another location, especially when they migrate great distances north or south. **This behaviour saves considerable energy, and the eagles hardly have to flap their wings.**"[20]

It's a great visual, for cool composure! When I imagine an eagle I don't ever visualize this captivating bird frantically flapping its wings with angst, trying to get ahead.

People who don't know God and the way he works FUSS... but you know both God and how he works. Steep your life in God-reality, God-initiative, God-provisions. Don't worry...

(Matthew 6:33 MSG)

That is just the wrong picture for such a majestic bird as the eagle. Who with great poise just stretches out his wings with ease and takes to the wind with elegant grace.

Very Little Energy

Even though the eagle can reach altitudes of over 10,000 feet, they are usually soaring to these heights, and taking long glides to cover ground, then soaring up again and repeating the process.

By flying in this way, their body is really not demanding much oxygen, not anywhere near as much as **when they are much closer to the ground and expending considerable energy flapping their wings.**[21]

When flying, **the bald eagle very rarely flaps its wings but soars instead,** holding its wings almost completely flat.[22]

From this we see that it's much easier for the eagle once it gets up into the heights. It expends less energy than when it's closer to the ground. Great aspect, because when we are soaring in the Spirit, depending less on the arm of the flesh, and more on Him, we don't tire so easily.

*But those who wait for the Lord [who expect, look for, and hope in Him] shall change **and** renew their strength **and** power; **THEY SHALL LIFT THEIR WINGS <u>AND</u> MOUNT UP [CLOSE TO GOD] AS EAGLES [MOUNT UP TO THE SUN];** they shall run and not be weary, they shall walk and not faint or become tired.*

(Isaiah 40:31 AMPC)

Obviously the spiritual implication from the bible's standpoint is that eagles actually rest in the heights. They don't over spend their energies staying on the ground. We could say that the more earth bound we are the more tired and weary we become. We were made to see things from Christ's perspective, to live from ABOVE and not from beneath.

STAY FOCUSED ON WHAT'S ABOVE, NOT ON EARTHLY THINGS.

(Colossians 3:2 VOICE)

*So if you're serious about living this new resurrection life with Christ, **act** like it. Pursue the things over which Christ presides.*

DON'T SHUFFLE ALONG, EYES TO THE GROUND, *absorbed with the things right in front of you.*

LOOK UP, *and be alert to what is going on around Christ –* **THAT'S WHERE THE ACTION IS. SEE THINGS FROM <u>HIS</u> PERSPECTIVE.**

(Colossians 3:1-4 MSG)

*If then you have been raised with Christ [to a new life, thus sharing His resurrection from the dead], **aim at and seek the [rich, eternal treasures] that are above, where Christ is,** seated at the right hand of God.*

*And **set your minds and keep them set on what is above (THE HIGHER THINGS), NOT ON THE THINGS THAT ARE ON THE EARTH.***

(Colossians 3:1-3 AMPC)

CHAPTER 14

The Trust Connection

Trust is Free but it's Not Cheap!

Eagles *(particularly the American Bald Eagle)* rigorously evaluate before trusting or making any connections *(covenant)*. We too should be more careful. **TRUST IS FREE BUT IT'S NOT CHEAP! It's both fragile and enduring and if nurtured properly can last forever – especially if it's not taken for granted!**

Eagles are big on this issue of trust. For example when a female eagle wants to test her mate, she allows him to pursue her up into the heights. But not before she swoops down and picks up a twig from the earth. With the male in hot pursuit, she reaches a great height before dropping the twig and watches as it falls.

The male hurtles after it at top speed, in order to catch it before it hits the ground. Returning it to the female, she then turns and flies to another altitude and repeats the process!

It is widely thought that she uses heavier twigs each time and at higher altitudes consecutively, meaning the level of difficulty increases with each test, until she is satisfied!

The Test of Dependability

We can call this a mating ritual. Nonetheless, it is a serious test of trust. A test of dependability and can go on for hours. Once the female eagle is **convinced that the male is dependable,** only then will she allow him to mate with her.

We too must test our commitments and connections. Not everything is what it seems or appears. Not all relationships will go the distance. So we must exercise some caution and seek God's will in each and every relationship.

A PERSON WHO WALKS BY THE SPIRIT EXAMINES EVERYTHING, sizing it up and seeking out truth. But no one is able to examine or size up that kind of spiritual person...
(1 Corinthians 2:15 VOICE)

BUT THE SPIRITUAL MAN TRIES ALL THINGS [HE EXAMINES, INVESTIGATES, INQUIRES INTO, QUESTIONS, AND DISCERNS ALL THINGS], yet is himself to be put on trial and judged by no one [he can read the meaning of everything, but no one can properly discern or appraise or get an insight into

*him]… we have the mind of Christ (the Messiah) and do
hold the thoughts (feelings and purposes) of His heart.*
(1 Corinthians 2:15-16 AMPC)

Their courtship behaviour can also include spectacular sky-dancing where the birds lock talons from great heights and then free fall through the air *(locked together),* separating just short of hitting the ground!

Incidentally eagles will usually stay with the same mate for life *(unless one dies)* and will nest at the same location, year after year. So **commitment, loyalty and dependability are high on the eagle's agenda** *(towards its mate and offspring).*

The moral of the story is this: saying, **"I LOVE YOU"** means **"YOU CAN DEPEND ON ME."** This is a big lesson for all of us. And love has many qualities to it, not just sexual attraction or emotional fixation.

Perfect love casteth out fear [of punishment but even betrayal or abandonment].
(1 John 4:18 emphasis added)

Charity never faileth.
(1 Corinthians 13:8)

Something that never fails can be depended upon. Love fits the bill. Only God can help us to walk in the God kind of love, towards Him and towards each other.

The love walk is high moral ground, where only the committed can walk or fly. **EVERYTHING IS SHORT-LIVED WITHOUT LOVE! Only love gives us the edge,** longevity or the *staying-power* that's required for any relationship.

CHAPTER 15

The Mentoring Concept

Time to Practise His Ability

It is considered myth for eagles to catch their young in mid-air as scripture suggests. But the symbolic meaning of scripture must be interpreted spiritually.

As an eagle stirs up its nest, hovers over its young, spreading out its wings, taking them up, **carrying them on its wings,** *so the LORD alone led him, and there was no foreign god with him.*

(Deuteronomy 32:11-12 NKJV)

The first Biblical reference to the eagle referred to the right bird. Exodus 19:4, *"Ye have seen what I did unto the Egyptians, and how* **I bare you on eagles' wings,** *and brought you unto myself."*

This "bare you on eagles' wings..." must not be interpreted to mean that an eagle ever carried anything on its back. It merely means that by strength of powerful wing it could carry quite a load with its feet and frequently was seen doing this. Vultures never carried anything; they feasted and regurgitated what they had eaten to their young.[23]

Eaglets are actually heavier than their parents when ready to fly! So the adult eagles do not carry them at all. But both their parents are active participants in raising them, both take responsibility to ensure that the parenting and mentoring process is a success.

Everything in its Time

Eagles are dictated to by seasons, such as migration and so on, therefore they will also instinctively know when it's time for their young to fledge *(be capable of flight)*. Obviously this includes the right plumage.

Everything in its right time and season is beautiful: *"God has made everything fit beautifully in its appropriate time..." (Ecclesiastes 3:11 NET)*

When the time comes they won't allow their young to languish in the nest, but will mentor them to get out of the nest and have a life of their own!

When an eagle is too fearful to leave, **a parent will sometimes withhold food to force it out.** This is being cruel to be kind. Without such tough love, the eagle will die. Sometimes we feel that God is withholding from us, and in those seasons we must seek God for fresh direction. It's uncomfortable. Inconvenient for the standards of our flesh but totally necessary for our development!

True mentorship will not create dependence but independence. Just as comfort-zones *(false security)* can become very uncomfortable, so can a nest especially if it's full of over-grown fledglings!

"Sometimes the adults will force the eaglets to fly. When chicks leave the nest they usually glide to a nearby tree or stump, **returning to the nest tree frequently and continuing to be fed by the adults.** At first the eaglets have difficulty landing on tree limbs.

However, if they land on the ground, they need open space to flap their wings to become airborne. **While eaglets improve their landing and flying skills, they depend on their parents for food.** The adults will bring food to where the eaglets are perched.

Eaglets will stay close to the nest and nest tree during the first few weeks after fledging. Within one month after fledging, eaglets will soar and drift over the water."[24]

This gives a perfect picture of the eagle's ability to nurture and not abandon their young, even once they have left the nest. Eagles are territorial and will naturally venture out for themselves. Adult parents don't tolerate overdependence. When a season comes to an end, everyone must move on.

"The eaglets are poor hunters and… **as the chicks develop their flight skills they harass the adults and try to take fish from them.** This behaviour helps eaglets learn to forage and be **independent** and will last into September.

At 17 to 23 weeks of age, the bond between the adults and their young fades and the adults no longer tolerate harassment from their offspring. This is time when the young eagles leave the territory, following the prevailing winds to more northerly shorelines and water bodies in search of good feeding grounds."[25]

Powerful Gentleness

Research has revealed that of all the bird family, none is more gentle and attentive to its young than the eagle. So the eaglets are not just thrown out of the nest as some suppose. There is a much more precise process that occurs.

They are reared, nurtured and mentored *(to succeed in the proper environment),* for which they were made and then encouraged to leave; to get on with their own lives. **This is true of discipleship. We are mentored to GO, not to STAY!**

> *He said to them, **GO** INTO ALL THE WORLD and preach **and** publish openly the good news (the Gospel) to every creature [of the whole human race].*
> *(Mark 16:15 AMPC)*

True mentorship is not about surviving but thriving. Having a long, successful life in the correct environment, eating the right food and knowing what to do, when and how to do it. This is the true purpose of mentoring.

Note: In scripture eagles are very symbolic *(prophetically speaking)* and there are over 30 different verses that refer to the great bird.

CHAPTER 16

Imprinting and Bonding

Following My Example

Eagles observe their parents. They learn to fly and to hunt by watching and then imitating them. For some creatures such things come instinctively but for the eagle he learns through what Konrad Lorenz discovered as "Imprinting."

> Pattern yourselves after me [follow my example], as I imitate **and** follow Christ (the Messiah).
>
> (1 Corinthians 11:1 AMPC)

> So imitate me, **watch my ways, follow my example,** just as I, too, **always seek** to imitate the Anointed One.
>
> (VOICE)

Through this process called **imprinting,** young birds **learn** to identify with their own species *(their instincts have to be developed).* For example, if eagles are raised with turkeys, they will grow up thinking *(behaving as if)* they are turkeys instead of eagles! Imprinting is not exclusive to eagles of course. Other animals are affected by this concept and if raised in captivity some animals can even believe that they are human!

Imprinted Behaviours

American Eagle Foundation bring clarity to this by saying, "At birth baby eagles go through a process known as imprinting, where **they instinctively become attached to the first moving object that regularly attends to their needs.**

Through imprinting, young birds learn to identify with their own species. During this period, the tiny eagle learns specific behaviours and habits it needs to survive. **For bald eagles, this critical period is from nine days to six weeks of age.**

Until it is nine days old, the chick's eyes cannot focus well enough to distinguish humans from mother eagles. However, from nine days and up to about six weeks of age, **the baby chick will imprint on a human if the human appears to be its food source.**

If this happens, the eagle will be permanently imprinted on that person or humans in general. This causes the eagle to look for humans to provide food. Possibly a worse result is that, once mature, the imprinted eagle will refuse to mate with other bald eagles."[26]

Learned Behaviour

This describes such a vulnerable season in the life of an eaglet, impressionable and open to hurt. Not unlike new-born believers who must have adequate role models to imitate. In this way they can learn to thrive.

In the world of psychology there is such a notion as *learned-behaviour, (including behaviourism and conditioning)*. Learned-behaviour is simple and is very much like imprinting. In Christendom, this is something that I have come to recognise and witness all over the world.

Unfortunately if new-born-believers are not spiritually birthed in the right way or placed in right environments *(healthy churches etc.)* to grow and be established, where faith is strong and the Holy Spirit is allowed to operate freely, they will only know how to mimic religion *(in all its shapes and forms!)*

Pseudo or Genuine

I'm not just talking about High Anglican or Catholic churches now either. I have been into some very prophetic churches *(at least they consider themselves as such)* only to see young believers getting caught up in some crazy stuff. Not being led of the Holy Spirit, but copying those deemed more spiritual. There's room to learn. But what are you learning?

Countless clips exist on the Internet showing very small children *(even babies)* swaying, raising hands, and appearing to be lost in worship. Of course this is touching but it is still a learned behaviour. They have watched their parents and mimicked the same.

It's adorable – even our own children have mimicked us. Our son used to hold church services in his bedroom with all his teddies and they'd all get saved and slain in the Spirit!

Just like he saw in church. How awesome. However when children get older, we must help them distinguish between genuine worship, *(derived from a personal relationship with God)*, and a basic learned behaviour.

> When I was a child, I spake as a child, I understood as a child, I thought as a child: but when I became a man, **I put away childish things.**
>
> *(1 Corinthians 13:11)*

This is discernable in churches across the globe. Much of what goes on is learned-behaviour, which is not wrong in a sense, but it does become a problem when people are prevented from having an authentic experience.

Either people are having a genuine encounter with God or they are not. As pastors and leaders we must watch for this, in order to help them cross from the pseudo over to the genuine. Yet if we don't notice the difference, then how will they?

We can fill up our seats and brag on numbers, but I ask you, **how many of those people are having a genuine experience with the living God and not a fake one?** Remembering that spiritual immaturity can readily perceive that which is only *simulated* as being the real thing.

Assumption vs. Knowledge

For example, an untrained eye will see no value in a twenty-four-carat gold ring, compared to nine-carat. It looks far too yellow for someone who is unaccustomed and has only ever worn nine-carat gold! In this case the expensive is perceived as cheap and vice-versa.

It too is a type of conditioning, for in certain countries, nothing less than twenty-four-carat gold is considered authentic, because it is more pure. But the downside to this is that the purer the gold, the softer it is.

Nine-carat gold on the other hand is considered the workingman's gold, because it is much harder and more durable. It has more parts other metals than gold, to make it harder. This affects its colour; in addition it is much cheaper.

Another modern day phenomena: cheap foods are much tastier today than their more expensive alternative. Simply because modern flavour enhancers such as MSG and others have so excited our taste buds that we prefer cheap, poor quality and highly marketed foods over fresh and high quality versions of the same. Without knowledge surely we perish!

My people are DESTROYED from LACK OF KNOWLEDGE.

(Hosea 4:6 NIV)

Such random examples indicate how easy it is to be conditioned *(to things, people, environment, culture etc.)* and

through familiarity make many assumptions about life without having any real knowledge.

This is where revelation must be a vital part of our lives. To strip back the ignorance and reveal things as they really are.

Imprinting and conditioning happens everywhere, including and especially in spiritual environments like church!

At the end of the day, people will mimic what they are continually exposed to. We need to ensure that we as believers are not exposed to religion but exposed regularly to the glory of God instead.

CHAPTER 17

What Do You See?

Too Fat to Fly

In an earlier chapter I mentioned growing up on the farm and how turkeys were lazy and reluctant fliers. The reason for this is because farmed turkeys have been so conditioned to their surroundings, and never develop the instinct to fly.

"While the turkey you cook for Thanksgiving [or *Christmas]* **has never been airborne, wild turkeys can fly...** not fast or high enough however... Wild turkeys feed on the ground, which may have something to do with the myth that they can't fly. They have to fly, however, because they roost in trees at night...

The Thanksgiving turkey... is so grossly fattened up on the farm that it has about as much chance of flying as you do after your pumpkin pie."[27]

Likewise we can be so conditioned and limited to our surroundings, when God has so much more for us. Our conditioning has to change. What we see must change.

Our perceptions are very important because we are bound by what we see *(or don't see)*. Unless the image changes, then we too will be like the baby eagle, which is vulnerable to false imprinting. It's not overstating it to say that our entire future depends on what we see, in terms of vision.

Vision

As much as scripture declares that without knowledge God's people perish, they also perish for the lack of vision. Let's take a look at the following scripture, "Where there is no vision, the people perish..." *(Proverbs 29:18)* from different versions of the bible:

Where there is no <u>REVELATION</u>, people cast off restraint... (NIV)

When <u>PROPHECY</u> faileth, the people shall be destroyed... (WYC)

Without a <u>VISION</u> is a people made NAKED... (YLT)

<u>IF PEOPLE CAN'T SEE</u> WHAT GOD IS DOING, THEY STUMBLE ALL OVER THEMSELVES; but when they attend to what he <u>REVEALS</u>, they are most blessed. (MSG)

WITHOUT PROPHETIC <u>VISION</u> PEOPLE RUN WILD... *(GW)*

Pretty conclusive! Sight, revelation, prophetic scope in our lives, is our lifeline. This is what conditions us to the will of God rather than the will of man *(self will or our foe)*?

Let the Reformed Say So

Do not ye be conformed to this world, **BUT BE YE <u>REFORMED</u> IN NEWNESS OF YOUR WIT...**
(Romans 12:2 WYC)

Formative years shape us. In fact we are affected by those years for the rest of our lives. Similarly, as people of God, our spiritual development is critical.

BE... TRANSFORMED BY THE RENEWING OF YOUR MIND...
(Romans 12:2)

FIX YOUR ATTENTION ON GOD. You'll be changed from the inside out. Readily recognize what he wants from you, and quickly respond to it.
(Romans 12:2 MSG)

I have always liked the words REFORMATION, REGENERATION, AND TRANSFORMATION; they say everything about what Christ did for us. He wiped our slate clean.

All the old conditioning *(imprinting)* of our past lives *(no matter how misfortunate)* is all wiped away. In Christ all things become new and the old is washed away.

*Therefore if any man be in Christ, **HE IS A <u>NEW</u> CREATURE: <u>OLD THINGS ARE PASSED AWAY</u>; BEHOLD, <u>ALL</u> THINGS ARE BECOME <u>NEW</u>.***
(2 Corinthians 5:17)

*Therefore if any person is [ingrafted] in Christ (the Messiah) **HE IS A <u>NEW CREATION</u> (A NEW CREATURE ALTOGETHER);** the old [previous moral and spiritual condition] has passed away. **Behold, the fresh <u>and</u> new has come!***
(2 Corinthians 5:17 AMPC)

*Anyone united with the Messiah **GETS A FRESH START, IS <u>CREATED NEW</u>. THE OLD LIFE IS <u>GONE</u>;** a new life burgeons!*
(2 Corinthians 5:17 MSG)

This is how we can be totally reconditioned. More than that - "CREATED NEW." "THE OLD LIFE IS GONE." This is how abuse victims can go free! They don't have to endure a life sentence. They can get cleaned up from the inside out through Christ and possess a different image of their heavenly Father, *(than their earthly one provided for them).*

Free from Brokenness

Hurting people, hurt people. Abused people, abuse people. It's a cycle that only salvation through Christ can break. Where psychology can only identify the problem *(brokenness)*, Christ solves it and sets the captives *(victims)* free once and for all.

*The Spirit of the Lord God is upon me; because the Lord hath anointed me to preach good tidings unto the meek; he hath sent me **to bind up the brokenhearted,** to proclaim liberty to the captives, and the opening of the prison to them that are bound...*

(Isaiah 61:1)

That's how abuse victims can be changed forever and set free of their pain, rather than perpetuate it to the next generation.

Christ Breaks the Curse

For one example, it has long been recognised that sons, who see their fathers beating their mothers and sisters, often make covenants within their own hearts, to vow that they will never treat women the same way.

Yet they grow up only to perpetuate the exact behaviour they were exposed to and programmed by. Not even their early abhorrence had the power to dislocate them from the impulse to mimic such.

Imprinting therefore has evidently played a very powerful part in all our lives, for good and for bad; not one of us has been exempt or immune.

Even early legends and fables spoke of lost children being raised by the wolf pack *(for example)* and exhibited animal rather than human instincts, as a result. So imprinting has not been a new concept and has fascinated people for very many generations.

This is why when we come to Christ, we must be broken free from all other influences in our lives and become new creations.

CHAPTER 18

Maturation & Independence

Revelation Gives You the Ability

As the eaglet must learn to fly and hunt for himself, so must we. Hunt daily for our own revelation, the fresh *(daily)* meat of God's Word. Fresh, not spiritual carrion *(toxic road kill!)* We must gather our own manna to grow and to stay healthy and strong in our Christian walk.

As I have already mentioned, mentors should help feed young believers until they can feed themselves; developing their own skills and making their own choices in life *(to succeed on their own merits)*.

> *Train up a child in the way he should go [and in keeping with his individual gift or bent], and **when he is old he will not depart from it.***
>
> *(Proverbs 22:6 AMPC)*

Teach a child how to follow the right way; even when he is old, **he will stay on course.**

(VOICE)

My son, listen thou to thy father's teaching; and do not thou abandon thy mother's principles; *so that grace be added... increased, so that favour be added unto thee, and a band of honour be put about thy neck.*

(Proverbs 1:8-9 WYC)

Until we all attain oneness in the faith and in the comprehension of the [full and accurate] knowledge of the Son of God, **that [we might arrive] at really mature manhood** *(the completeness of personality which is nothing less than the standard height of Christ's own perfection), the measure of the stature of the fullness of the Christ* **and** *the completeness found in Him.*

(Ephesians 4:13 AMPC)

Driven by Spiritual Hunger

Hunger drives an eaglet from the nest. It is not thrown from the nest. There is a coaxing from the parents. Where the young can develop the understanding that the nest is no longer a safe place to remain. Starvation has now made it a dangerous and uncomfortable environment.

The season has switched. The young eagle must recognize that something has changed. Otherwise it will return to the nest looking for food, where there is none.

Teasing the young with food helps them come to this decision! Far from being programmed with abandonment issues, the young eagle is taught intelligent strategies very early on.

Stripped Back to Move On

Not only does the nest start to represent hunger, loneliness and discomfort, it is also cold and unwelcoming. When our surroundings change for the worse, sometimes this forces change in our lives that must happen anyway! It's not the devil. It is all part of God's mentoring process.

I have often called this stage **"being stripped back."** When it seems that everything is being taken away from you, in order to get you to move to the next level. Even Paul the great apostle was not immune to this mode of development:

> *I know what it is to be in need, and I know what it is to have plenty.* ***I HAVE LEARNED THE SECRET OF BEING CONTENT IN ANY AND EVERY SITUATION,*** *whether well fed or hungry, whether living in plenty or in want.*
>
> *(Philippians 4:12 NIV)*

When life's comfortable, there's no need to go elsewhere. Especially when the food supply is rich and abundant and regularly supplied! Why move? All animals are creatures of comfort to some degree. They will dwell where their basic needs are being met: safety, food and shelter.

Still an eaglet must go through a stage of metamorphosis, from a place where it is *being fed* to a place where it can *feed itself.*

Naturally this is a progressive journey; no baby is left to fend for itself for it will die. A young eaglet must learn to hunt for itself, relatively quickly or it will starve.

Remember, "Champions never become champions, with losing information. You can't duplicate another's success, until you can duplicate another's knowledge. You will have to be connected to the same sources of information as those ahead of you, before you can reach those ahead of you. 'Uncommon Information' never comes from an 'Average Source.'"[28]

CHAPTER 19

When the Brook Dries Up

His Ways are Not Ours

In my own personal walk with the Lord, particularly during the first years of being full time in the ministry and living totally by faith *(without a regular wage or any other source of income)* I soon learnt when it was time to move on. The brook would dry up!

Eventually the brook dried up because of the drought. Then God spoke to him: "GET UP AND GO to Zarephath in Sidon and live there. I'VE INSTRUCTED A WOMAN WHO LIVES THERE, A WIDOW, TO FEED YOU."
(1 Kings 17:7-9 MSG)

If God moved on, then I would have to move on too! This is how God taught me to follow the leading of His Spirit and not just my own appetites, desires or wishes to provide for myself.

I learnt that when God pays the bills - you could no longer call the shots! *"The just shall live by faith: but if any man draw back, my soul shall have no pleasure in him" (Hebrews 10:38).*

When God says, "Get up and go!" It's time to go! There's no use arguing. The circumstances won't change to suit me but to suit God's purposes in my life.

In addition not everybody's training is identical. God has different purposes for each of us. But what we can never neglect or overlook, is the fact that we are called according to **His purposes and not our own.**

*We are assured **and** know that [God being a partner in their labor] all things work together **and** are [fitting into a plan] for good to **and FOR THOSE WHO LOVE GOD AND ARE CALLED ACCORDING TO [HIS] DESIGN AND PURPOSE.***
(Romans 8:28 AMPC)

*We are confident that God is able to orchestrate everything to work toward something good **and beautiful** when we love Him and **ACCEPT HIS INVITATION TO LIVE ACCORDING TO HIS PLAN.***
(VOICE)

God always has another plan and you don't want to miss what He is doing or get stuck in a past season where His provision and anointing has long vacated!

Breaking the Bond

For the eaglet it is the same, there is no going back. In a quickly changing environment the eaglet discovers that not only is his nest slowly being dismantled and his food supply being cut off, but also he is steadily loosing weight. The only purpose behind it all is that the eaglet deliberately abandons the nest of his own accord and wills himself to move on in life, without being pushed. A new season of change to propel him into his destiny!

People who don't want to help themselves can't be helped. If they have to be pushed now, they will always need coaxing to succeed, which is dysfunctional. God desires us to be free, not needy and bound.

If the parents wanted to keep the eaglets bound to the nest, all they'd be required to do is keep the supply coming *(by conveyor belt!)* but an overdependence in the young eagles, would mean certain death for both parent and young.

Therefore the parents use food as leverage now instead, to tease the young from their nest and systematically begin starving them, in order that they develop such an overpowering hunger, that it drives them from their nest.

They arrive at a place where they *voluntarily* break the bond with their last season! Their need forces their own decision, even if they were helped to make it!

At one point the young eaglets is a little heavier than his parents, but now is leaner, lighter and firm-muscled *(and more easily picked by the updraft when he eventually stretches his wings!)*

So not everything is what it seems! What might seem like starvation and cruelty at first is all part of a larger plan. Preparation for the young eagles' first flight, helping him be ready for his first ride on the updrafts. Just as he sees his parents doing, who fly past his nest regularly with food, enticing him to fly.

As soon as the young eagle lifts up on the wind, airborne for the first time, he glides haphazardly to the nearest branch. Catching his bearing, he looks for his parents, who quickly swoop to give him his first reward *(food!)*

Prepared for the Unthinkable!

Our hunger for the Lord is created through different circumstances, and leads us to do the unthinkable! But oh how glorious it is when we take our first flight on the winds of God's Holy Spirit!

When we are young *(just born again)*, meat seams to drop from the heavens. Everything is so easy. But when we come of age, God demands much more from us.

FOR UNTO WHOMSOEVER MUCH IS GIVEN, OF HIM SHALL BE MUCH REQUIRED: and to whom men have committed much, of him they will ask the more.
(Luke 12:48)

It's important for us to realise that when it's time to come of age spiritually, God will not make things easy for us. He will always be present, but won't always rescue.

The following lyrics describe a believer who recognises his need for God. To be treated like the eaglet – released from the old, into the new. Broken of self-will in order to be free:

Make me broken
So I can be healed
'Cause I'm so calloused
And now I can't feel
I want to run to You
With heart wide open
Make me broken
Make me empty
So I can be filled
'Cause I'm still holding
Onto my will
And I'm completed
When You are with me
Make me empty

Chorus
'Til You are my one desire
'Til You are my one true love
'Til You are my breath, my everything
Lord, please keep making me
Make me lonely
So I can be Yours
'Til I want no one
More than You, Lord
'Cause in the darkness
I know You will hold me
Make me lonely[29]

CHAPTER 20

Eagles are Strategists

Source of Power

Remarkably the Golden Eagle will prey on animals much larger than itself and won't readily surrender to his prey's opposing strength or size. For example, this eagle will literally drag a goat off the side of a cliff, which is more a display of his incredible hunting strategy, than of its physical prowess *(muscle or strength)*.

In addition to this, it is not afraid to fight for its prey or for its territory. This makes eagles all round fearless: hunters, defenders and providers.

I suggest to you that all mature spiritual eagles should work strategically. With age and development comes wisdom.

Once we learn to operate out of wisdom *(other than bravado, ego, charisma, raw energy or testosterone)* we have discovered what it means to no longer trust in the arm of the flesh. This is why the mature usually see more results, because they are usually strategy driven and not ego or self driven.

> *This is what the Lord says: "Cursed is the one who trusts in man, who* **DRAWS STRENGTH FROM MERE FLESH** *and whose heart turns away from the Lord."*
>
> *(Jeremiah 17:5 NIV)*

> *Cursed is the person who trusteth in people, and* **MAKETH ANY FLESH HIS SOURCE OF POWER AND SECURITY,** *and his heart goeth away from the Lord.*
>
> *(Jeremiah 17:5 WYC)*

> *We can be strong and courageous because of the One who fights with us. Don't be discouraged or fearful of the Assyrian king and the multitude of his people, for greatness is with us more than with them.*
>
> **SENNACHERIB WILL FIGHT WITH AN ARM OF FLESH AND BONE,** *but we will fight with the Eternal God's help and His warfare. The people were strengthened...*
>
> *(2 Chronicles 32:7-8 VOICE)*

> **AN ARM OF FLESH IS WITH HIM;** *but the Lord our God is with us, he is our helper, and shall fight for us. And the people were encouraged...*
>
> *(2 Chronicles 32:8 WYC)*

People who have matured in God, work less in their own strength and are more reliant and dependant on God. Some of us learn this sooner than others, but the arm of the flesh fails. Once we step over into mature strategy, we experience fewer confrontations with the devil *(in other words we make less mistakes!)* Immature believers are always fighting devils - have you ever noticed?

When they figure out that the biggest enemy they face is themselves, they'll calm down, start depending on strategy, wisdom and revelation, securing better results; *(brute force, intelligence and human calculation, will always be folly, in the shadow of God's surpassing wisdom!)*

I often like to paraphrase this particular scripture for the same reason: "Faith without STRATEGY is dead!"

*As the body without the spirit is dead, so **FAITH WITHOUT WORKS IS DEAD...***

(James 2:26)

REMOVING ACTION [STRATEGY] FROM FAITH IS LIKE REMOVING BREATH FROM A BODY. ALL YOU HAVE LEFT IS A CORPSE.

(James 2:26 VOICE [strategy] added)

How to Develop Personal Strategy

How? Well let me help you put this into practice in your own life. We must get the patterns from heaven like Moses did. God is our only source and supply – who knows our - here and now – better than we do.

If we are honest, everyone wants a formula. We all do. But it's just not that easy and it's not meant to be. Yet, absolutes do exist, things that God has set that will never alter. Such as the ROCK, **the foundation of our lives and ministries will always be built upon the ROCK.**

These words I speak to you are not incidental additions to your life, homeowner improvements to your standard of living.

THEY ARE FOUNDATIONAL WORDS, WORDS TO BUILD A LIFE ON. If you work these words into your life, you are like a smart carpenter who built his house on solid rock.

Rain poured down, the river flooded, a tornado hit – but NOTHING MOVED THAT HOUSE. IT WAS FIXED TO THE ROCK.

(Matthew 7:24 MSG)

CHAPTER 21

The Rock of Revelation

The Ultimate Plan

Jesus told Peter that He would build the Church upon the **rock of revelation** and how the gates of hell would not prevail against that revelation - specifically concerning who Christ was: "Messiah, the Son of the living God."

*Simon Peter answered, "**You are the Messiah, the Son of the living God.**" Jesus replied, "Blessed are you, Simon son of Jonah, for **THIS WAS NOT <u>REVEALED</u> TO YOU BY FLESH AND BLOOD, BUT BY MY FATHER IN HEAVEN.***

*And I tell you that you are Peter, and **ON THIS ROCK I WILL BUILD MY CHURCH,** and the gates of Hades will not overcome it."*

(Matthew 16:16-18 NIV)

When we have a clear view of who Christ is, and what He has commissioned us to do, with revelation, we can then move forwards knowing that the gates of hell will not prevail.

Whenever I am on an aeroplane I enjoy the part where we break through above the clouds. How serene it is up there above the clouds and smog and cares of life.

If I were an eagle I would spend much of my time up there! I would go there to think straight, to get away, and to have a clear head closer to the sun. Likewise, we too can soar in the Spirit and get clear revelation, if we will go where the revelation is!

Religious Formulas

So, can we live by revelation or by formula? If we give ourselves to random formulas, we'll just become religious and irrelevant. It's all too easy to become religious with all of our man-made formulas. There is a difference between structure and formula, although both can be man-made.

> *They're full of FORMULAS and programs and advice, PEDDLING TECHNIQUES for getting what you want from God. Don't fall for that nonsense.*
> (Matthew 6:10 MSG)

We are given clear instructions in scripture on how to run our lives; how to administrate the affairs of Church life and our home lives, from marriage and raising children, to how we must keep order in our meetings and honour leadership; so on and so forth. All in all, Christianity is not an emotional-free-for-all.

"We were designed to rule like God rules — in generosity and kindness, not self-serving, but always for the higher good of others. We are to rule over creation, over darkness — that we might plunder the powers of darkness and establish the rule of Jesus wherever we go preaching the Gospel of the Kingdom.

Kingdom means 'King's domain.' In the original purpose of God, humankind was to rule over creation. But then sin entered our domain, refining our talks to that which affects eternity. Because of sin, creation has been infected by darkness — disease, sickness, afflicting spirits, poverty, natural disasters, demonic influence, etc.

Intended Fruit

While our rule is still over creation, it has become focused on exposing and undoing the works of the devil. That is the ministry of Jesus that we inherited in His commission. That is the intended fruit of the Christian life. If I have a power encounter with God, which we are required to pursue, then I am equipped to give it away to others.

This is the ministry of Jesus — use the power and authority of God to carry on the ministry of Jesus, in the way that Jesus did it. The invasion of God into impossible situations comes through a people who have received power from on high and have learned to release it into the circumstances of life.

The heart of God is for partnership with His created likeness. He's the ultimate King who loves to empower. His heart from day one was to have a people who lived like Him, loved like Him, created and ruled like Him. From day one,

God's desire has been to be with His creation as the invited Landlord to look over their increased capacity to rule, making this world like His.

In His world, His glory is the center. The more people carry His Presence into all the earth as joyful servants of the Most High, the more we will be positioned to see one of Heaven's major mile markers—the earth covered with the glory of the Lord."[30]

Time on the Mountaintop

However strategy is something that we can get straight from the Lord, both individually and corporately, but we have to go to the mountaintop to obtain it like Moses did. It's not necessarily something we'll get from the pages of our Logos, but by the Rhema. Hearing the VOICE of God or the Singular Sayings of God... then repeating with our lips the things God has said which we believe with our hearts.

Moses was building the tabernacle, and God made sure that he was building according to the patterns that came from heaven and not his own. We too must get our patterns from God. An Old Testament theme that is remembered in the New Testament, therefore we must apply it to our lives:

> *They serve at a sanctuary that is a copy and shadow of what is in heaven. This is why Moses was warned when he was about to build the tabernacle:* ***"See to it that you MAKE EVERYTHING ACCORDING TO THE PATTERN SHOWN YOU ON THE MOUNTAIN."***
> *(Hebrews 8:5 NIV)*

Be careful to do it exactly as you saw it on the Mountain.
(Hebrews 8:5 MSG)

Often people ask me how to build a ministry but you can't just give people ministries. They can become part of one and learn how to live with clear boundaries. But even when learning to live within a set of boundaries, all of us still need to know how to be led of the Spirit within those boundaries.

This is why you need to know how to hear His Voice, what's sown in your heart will become your future!

Profitable Instruction

All scripture is given by inspiration of God, and is profitable for doctrine, for reproof, for correction, for instruction in righteousness.
(2 Timothy 3:16)

There's nothing like the written Word of God for showing you the way to salvation through faith in Christ Jesus. **Every part of Scripture is God-breathed and useful one way or another** – *showing us truth, exposing our rebellion, correcting our mistakes,* **training us to live God's way.** *Through the Word we are put together and shaped up for the tasks God has for us.*
(2 Timothy 3:16 MSG)

I have always said that we learn by instruction, such as imitating Paul; leaders who help us make the right decisions and choices in life, based on what they have learnt. Christianity is not all about being caught up in the Spirit and doing whatever we want, something that can be fuelled with rebellion and just lead to flakiness.

> **THE KINGDOM OF HEAVEN IS LIKE A DRAGNET** *which was cast into the sea and gathered in fish of every sort.*
>
> *When it was full, men dragged it up on the beach, and sat down and sorted out the good fish into baskets, but the worthless ones they threw away.*
>
> (Matthew 13:47-48 AMPC)

Then there is Networking; which is a working together in God's vineyard. There must be a working together, so that we can help take the strain of the net together, in order to catch the fish. Then in addition to networking, there are the five-fold gifts that must also work together.

> *He handed out gifts above and below, filled heaven with his gifts, filled earth with his gifts.* **HE HANDED OUT GIFTS OF APOSTLE, PROPHET, EVANGELIST, AND PASTOR-TEACHER TO TRAIN CHRIST'S FOLLOWERS** *in skilled servant work, working within Christ's body, the church,* **until we're all moving rhythmically and easily with each other,** *efficient and graceful in response to God's Son, fully mature adults, fully developed within and without, fully alive like Christ.*
>
> (Ephesians 4:11-12 MSG)

CHAPTER 22

Legend or Myth

Renewed Like the Eagle!

One of the most fascinating stories *(that has no scientific foundation)* is that of the aging eagle. Based on the following scripture that tells us our youth can be **"renewed like the eagle's."**

*Bless the LORD, O my soul, And forget not all His benefits: Who forgives all your iniquities, Who heals all your diseases, Who redeems your life from destruction, Who crowns you with lovingkindness and tender mercies, Who satisfies your mouth with good things, **SO THAT YOUR YOUTH IS RENEWED LIKE THE EAGLE'S.***

(Psalms 103:2-5 NKJV)

There are numerous mentions of eagles throughout scripture and many myths and legends surround the eagle. Many of which cannot be corroborated by expert facts! Most are based on fiction. I found countless faith based organizations teaching these myths as if they were facts. *(It would make great sermon material if it were true!)*

One such myth predicts that an aging eagle, in defiance of the aging process, will take itself off to a secluded spot, high up in the mountains *(at the end of its life span, approx. 20-30 years; longer if in captivity)* and plucks out all of its aging feathers. It remains hidden away from sight until all its feathers grow back renewed!

This would be fantastic if it were true! According to one source, the only problem with this particular myth is the fact that an eagle's feathers tend to grow back in patches, *(not as a complete coat)* and over a relatively long period of time. In addition, the bird would be very vulnerable to the elements and would die of starvation and thirst, long before its feathers ever grew back!

For example, one of many random bloggers wrote the following: "What is really interesting is that the eagle never gives up living, instead it retreats to a mountaintop and over a five month period goes through a metamorphosis. It knocks off its own beak by banging it against a rock, plucks out its talons and then feathers. Each stage produces a re-growth of the removed body parts, allowing the eagle to live for another 30 - 40 years."

Chinese Whispers

The funny thing about this myth is that it has been circulated online and re-written so many times that *the facts change with each writer!* A bit like the game "Chinese Whispers" that we played as children. And funnier still, *(this blogger did not think it through!)* but there could be no beak-less or talon-less bird alive *(of any kind)* that could successfully pluck out its own feathers!!

Without a beak, how would it achieve the task of plucking anything out? *(Hilarious!)* But on a more serious note, this was actually on a leadership-training website. Wow! How we must get our facts straight!

This particular blogger *(I choose to keep anonymous)* went on to suggest that this "renewed" eagle would then live another 40 years, till it was 70! Researching this matter however, I found no expert proof *(anywhere)*, to validate such claims - only the opposite!

A bird of prey living without feathers, talons or a beak would die of starvation and exposure. These birds live to approx. 30 years max, and a little longer in captivity. But not till 70!

"For those who are wondering if it's true that an aging eagle can go into seclusion, pluck out all of its feathers, shed its beak and talons, and then grow new ones in X number of days; subsequently, becoming renewed and living longer... It's a myth!

Science and Logic

…Both science and logic indicate an eagle cannot survive for any length of time without his or her feathers, beak and talons. Exposure and starvation would overcome the eagle long before a physical renewal could occur.

An eagle's beak and talons grow continuously, because they are made of keratin, the same substance as our hair and fingernails. Eagles molt in patches, taking almost half a year to replace feathers, starting with the head and working downward. Not all feathers are replaced in a given molt."[31]

"As the juvenile gets older, the bill will turn from dark brownish-black to yellow and the head and tail turn white… **BALD EAGLES CAN LIVE TO ABOUT 20-30 YEARS OF AGE IN THE WILD.** They live even longer in captivity. Bald eagles in the wild face a lot of threats that reduce their lifespan…"[32]

What can we take away from this? For me I always have to bring it back to scripture, to perceive what God is saying to us. One suggestion for any scriptural claim that our youth is **"renewed like the eagle's"** is perhaps due to the many phases of development that an eagle undergoes to reach maturity. Becoming visibly more majestic with age!

"IN THEIR FIVE-YEAR DEVELOPMENT TO ADULTHOOD, BALD EAGLES GO THROUGH ONE OF THE MOST VARIED PLUMAGE CHANGES OF ANY NORTH AMERICAN BIRD…

PROGRESSIVELY CHANGES UNTIL IT REACHES ADULT PLUMAGE AT FIVE YEARS... see how its beak changes form **grey-black to a VIBRANT YELLOW...** the white head and tail announce that it is of breeding age."[33]

Strength

Therefore when scripture says that, our strength is renewed like an eagle's, it's referring to a spiritual strength, a renewal. As the eagle's goes through an annual renewal. Without strong healthy feathers, an eagle is incapacitated.

Note: "Adults and immature birds have **one complete annual molt,** which is very gradual, and prolonged through spring, summer, and fall. The flight feathers are molted mainly during July, August, and September."[34]

CHAPTER 23

Final Word

The Road to Maturity

S piritual puberty is a subject that I've taught many times over the years, using a series, which I wrote, entitled, "The Road to Maturity." It can be an awkward phase in any of our lives but essential for our development. No one walks out of the womb or hits the ground running, the law of progression dictates that we can't run before we can walk.

Therefore **any part of the development process that is unnaturally forced or delayed, will create long-term dysfunction.** This development phase is a very vulnerable part of life that is aptly called the formative years. How well our adult life develops, is largely hinged on how we have reacted or handled the changes that we went through during that development time.

So, in addition, perhaps when scripture suggests that our youth is renewed like the eagle, it is because an eagle's stunning visage only unfolds with age.

Hans Christian Andersen's famous story, "The Ugly Duckling," used the narrative of an ugly duckling with clumsy immaturity eventually transforming into elegant beauty!

Likewise we in Christ are not to grow weary with age; we are to grow more elegant and beautiful, more secure, wise and radiant. All because of time well spent in and under the anointing, oiling our wheels and allowing our strength to be renewed.

The Secret of Resting and Renewal

Another reason that scripture says our youth is renewed like the eagle *(as mentioned in a previous chapter)* is that eagles lose energy very quickly and must preserve their energy at all costs. Even when flying, they will not use more energy than they have to.

Spiritual eagles learn the secret of RESTING in the Lord and not wearing themselves out living by pseudo and nervous energy that gets depleted quickly and can't be replenished. God alone is our source and supply.

> *YES, MY SOUL, FIND REST IN GOD; my hope comes from him.*
>
> *(Psalm 62:5 NIV)*

Two Types of Eagles

There are two types of eagles spiritually speaking: those who live close to the ground, using up too much energy *(the arm of the flesh) and who live like scavengers* on dead meat.

Then there are those who soar on the heights, use less of their own energy *(depending more on the Holy Spirit)* and don't grow weary. They get revelation from the third heaven *(clear sighted above the clouds)* and **remain healthy and strong by eating fresh prey *(revelation)* every single day.**

Have an Abundant Life.
Dr Alan

❖

Endnotes

References

1. Smith's Bible Dictionary, http://biblehub.com/topical/e/eagle. htm

2. YouTube Video Clip, http://youtube.com/watch?v=vEVd0QMjCc8

3. Prophets and Personal Prophecy Volume 1, God's Prophetic Voice Today (passages taken from page 11 and 13), by Dr Bill Hamon, Publisher: Destiny Image, USA, 1987

4. Healing and Deliverance, A Present Reality (page 45), by Dr Alan Pateman, Publisher: APMI Publications, 1994, Third Update: 2020

5. Prayers that Avail Much, Special Edition, by Word Ministries, Inc., Publisher: Harrison House, USA, 1989

6. Overcoming Crisis, the Secrets to Thriving in Challenging Times, by Myles Munroe, Publisher: Destiny Image, USA, 2009

7. http://whatdotheyeat.info/what-do-bald-eagles-eat © 2014 What Do They Eat? • Powered by WordPress & Mimbo

8. http://curiosity.discovery.com/question/what-franklins-view-national-symbol

9. Historical content is based on the official history of the Great Seal. Copyright ©2014 by John D. MacArthur, http://greatseal.com/symbols/turkey.html

10. http://homeofheroes.com/hallofheroes/1st_floor/flag/1bfc_eagle.html

11. http://utahflagman.blogspot.it/2011/01/u-s-presidents-flag.html

12. http://birding.about.com/od/Bird-Trivia/a/20-Fun-Facts-About-Vultures.htm

13. Healing and Deliverance, A Present Reality (page 123), by Dr Alan Pateman, Publisher: APMI Publications, 1994, Third Update: 2020

14. http://baldeagleinfo.com/eagle/eagle3.html

15. Feeding The Sick Raptor, http://gwexotics.com/wccms-resources/a/7/d/1/b83e271e-b766-11e0-a685-0050568626ea.pdf

16. Tongues, Our Supernatural Prayer Language (page 69), by Dr Alan Pateman, Publisher: APMI Publications, 2016

17. Charles H. Spurgeon

18. Yukozimo.com powered by WordPress, http://diet.yukozimo.com/what-do-eagles-eat

19. Natalie Waterworth, http://talentedheads.com/2013/04/09/generation-confused

20. Bald Eagle Facts Q&A with Peter Nye in 2007, http://learner.org/jnorth/tm/eagle/ExpertAnswer07.html

21. Bald Eagle Facts Q&A with Peter Nye in 2002 New York Department of Environmental Conservation, http://learner.org/jnorth/tm/eagle/ExpertAnswer02.html

22. http://defenders.org/bald-eagle/basic-facts

23. International Standard Bible Encyclopedia

24. U.S. Fish & Wildlife Service, http://fws.gov/uploadedFiles/Region_5/NWRS/Central_Zone/Montezuma/EagleFacts.pdf

25. U.S. Fish & Wildlife Service, http://fws.gov/uploadedFiles/Region_5/NWRS/Central_Zone/Montezuma/EagleFacts.pdf

26. American Eagle Foundation, http://eagles.org/vu-study/behaviors.php

27. Robert Roy Britt – Live Science, http://livescience.com/32229-can-turkeys-fly.html

28. You Were Born a Champion... Don't Die a Loser! The Secrets that Make Winners Win, by J. Konrad Hölè, Publisher: The World Press, USA, 1996, Revised Edition: 1998

29. Keep Making Me by Sidewalk Prophets, Album: Live Like That, Publishing: ©2012 Dayspring Music, LLC (BMI) / Simple Tense Songs, Wyzell Music (ASCAP), (Adm. by Simpleville Music), Writer(s): David Frey / Ben McDonald / Sam Mizell

30. Hosting the Presence, Unveiling Heaven's Agenda (pages 44-45), by Bill Johnson, Publisher: Destiny Image Publishers, Inc., USA, 2012

31. American Bald Eagle Information, Eagle Myths, Folklore and Legends, http://baldeagleinfo.com/eagle/eagle-myths.html

32. National Wildlife Foundation, http://nwf.org/wildlife/wildlife-library/birds/bald-eagle.aspx

33. Southwestern Bald Eagle Management Committee, Guiding Bald Eagle Management in Arizona, http://swbemc.org/plummage.html

34. American Eagle Foundation, http://americaneaglefoundation.wordpress.com/2011/03/11/how-do-the-feathers-of-bald-eagles-molt-and-change-color

Bible translations

Note: Where scriptures appear with special emphasis (in bold or italic) we have edited them ourselves in order to bring focused attention within the context of the subject being taught in this book.

❖

Ministry Profile

Since its inception in 1987 Alan Pateman Ministries *(a Christian-based Para church, non-profit and non-denominational outreach)* has developed across the globe, but now is focusing on three main areas:

1. "Connecting for Excellence" apostolic network. CFE is a multi-facetted missions organisation with the purpose of connecting leaders for divine opportunities and building lasting relationships. Apostle Alan has to date ordained more than 500 ministers in over 50 nations. In addition there are ministries, churches and schools who are in Association or Affiliation, looking to him to provide spiritual oversight, personal mentorship and accountability. Yearly conferences are being hosted *(where possible)* in different locations, to provide support and encouragement.

2. Secondly, the teaching arm, "LifeStyle International Christian University." Founded in 2007, LICU is a study program for students who desire to invest time from their lives into university studies where they can receive from the Anointing of the Word of God; not only to receive academic credits but an impartation that brings personal transformation. The same program can be applied for correspondence studies including identical syllabuses and study material designed for distance learning. Resulting in the same certification at the end of their studies! Degrees offered at our university range from a "Diploma in Theology" to a "Doctor of Philosophy" for those who decide to go through the full university program.

LICU is a global network of universities, operating from different nations *(overseeing correspondence students and local campuses)*, with national directors, faculty members and administrational staff who all relate to the International Head Office in Italy with the purpose of demonstrating the Supernatural Kingdom of God through Doctrinal, Apostolic and Prophetic Teaching. Yearly graduations are held in these nations *(such as Cameroon, the Netherlands, Italy and so on)*.

3. Media - known as an accomplished author and prolific writer, Dr Alan has published over eighty books *(to date)* and teaching materials, *(that have been made available in most formats)*. For example, his popular online **"Letters to the Churches"** called, Truth for the Journey, has developed a worldwide audience, including the newest venture, **Watchers of the 4 kings.**

To summarise, Dr Alan is Founder and President, CEO of **Alan Pateman Ministries International** (APMI), with his international Head Office in Italy that oversees national offices in different locations, and which umbrellas the following apostolic ministries:

- Connecting for Excellence Apostolic Network – Founder/ Overseer

- LifeStyle International Christian University - Dr Alan holds the position of President, CEO, Professor of Theology, Biblical Studies and Apostolic Ministry *(currently LICU is exploding throughout Europe, Asia and Africa)*

- International Apostolic Accreditation Council
- APMI Publishing and Publications / Media

On a personal note, Alan the family man, who grew up on an English farm, still enjoys long walks in the countryside with his family today. Still an avid walker, he spends many hours in the Tuscan hills and beautiful coastlines! Beyond his primary passions *(family and Christ)*, Alan has a very creative eye and innovative flare. As a talented artist, Alan loves painting large modern abstract canvases, but all forms of art and design are always stimulating to him, especially architecture and interior design. Not excluding the fact that Alan has always designed his own media materials, book covers and websites etc.

However, no matter how busy life gets, Dr Alan and his wife Jenny appreciate being surrounded by family and friends, children and growing number of grandchildren. They reside in Lucca, Tuscany *(The Eagle's Nest)*, Italy.

Alan Pateman Ph.D., D.Min., D.D., M.A., B.Th.

Note: The Eagle's Nest is a prophetic vision that God gave to Alan in 1996. He said, "Italy is your Nest *(Ministry International Head-Office)* and from it you will fly out, to and fro, to the nations."

Academic Background

Dr. Alan Pateman attended several colleges throughout his training *(including studying Theology at Roffey Place, Horsham, UK and a Member of Kerygma - with Rev. Colin Urquhart and Dr. Bob Gordon - 1985-1987)* before being awarded a Doctorate of Divinity *(2006)* in recognition of his lifetime achievements by the International College of Excellence, now "DanEl Christian College" *(President: Dr. Robb Thompson USA)* also "Life Christian University" *(Dr. Douglas Wingate USA)* where he also earned a Bachelor of Theology B.Th. *(2006)*, a Master of Arts in Theology M.A., a Doctor of Ministry in Theology D.Min., *(2007)* and Doctor of Philosophy in Theology Ph.D. *(2013)* from LICU.

❖

To Contact the Author

Please email:

Alan Pateman Ministries International

Email: apostledr@alanpateman.com
Web: www.AlanPatemanMinistries.com

*Please include your prayer requests
and comments when you write.*

❖
Other Books

Earnestly Contending for the State of Israel (End Times - Series Two)

The Jewish people are, and will continue to be God's people, He has not forgotten them or ever changed His mind where they are concerned. And now the time has come for the flag of Israel to be waved by the Jewish migrants who are gathering in their promised nation of Israel, today.

ISBN: 978-1-909132-71-9, Pages: 120, Format: Paperback, Published: 2018
Also available in eBook format!

Equipped for Spiritual Warfare

This book "Equipped for Spiritual Warfare" helps all believers and disciples of Christ to become warriors for these end times and to know where they belong… " Teaching you how to stand in His authority and dunamis power as an heir in Christ Jesus.

ISBN: 978-1-9091321-3-9, Pages: 148, Format: Paperback, Published: 2020
Also available in eBook format!

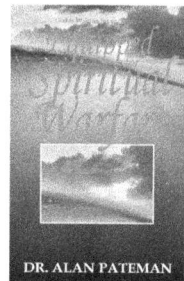

Truth for the Journey Books

His Faith Positions us for Possession

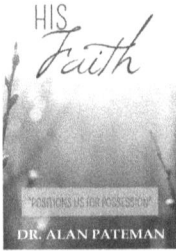

Within the pages of this book (which has to be a "must-read" for any serious enquirer into the Healing and Deliverance Ministry), Dr Alan unfolds a different pathway, so that the heartbeat of God's message of God's total deliverance can be released into the church of Jesus Christ today.

ISBN: 978-0-9570654-0-6, PAGES: 128, Format: Paperback, Published: 2014
Also available in eBook format!

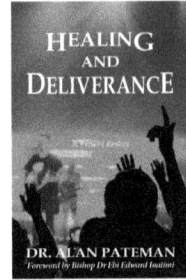

Healing and Deliverance, A Present Reality

Within the pages of this book (which has to be a "must-read" for any serious enquirer into the Healing and Deliverance Ministry), Dr Alan unfolds a different pathway, so that the heartbeat of God's message of God's total deliverance can be released into the church of Jesus Christ today.

ISBN: 978-1-909132-80-1, Pages: 188, Format: Paperback, First Print: 1994
Also available in eBook format!

Preparations for Ministry (Apostleship Series) Part Three

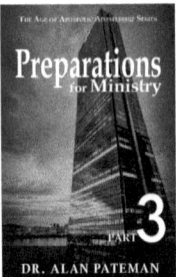

Preparations for Ministry is not something that many want to face. There is an expectation for a trophy for participation, but advice, oversight and years of preparation are necessary to achieve the goals that God has set before us.

ISBN: 978-1-909132-60-3, Pages: 128, Format: Paperback, Published: 2017
Also available in eBook format!

Dear Friends,

Have you considered becoming one of our international students? We are privileged to welcome you, from around the world, to "LifeStyle International Christian University" *(the teaching arm of Alan Pateman Ministries International).* **An English speaking university** dedicated to your success; to see you trained and equipped to fully succeed in your God given Destiny.

It is our passion to raise up the leaders of tomorrow, who will have influence in all realms of authority, including the Body of Christ. Men and women of strategy, wisdom and true godliness, who'll stand with stature and maturity in this hour.

It's undeniable that in today's world, recognised education has become indispensable, therefore it is our desire to offer well balanced and well structured courses. Those that have been written by gifted and talented ministers of God, who seek to be inspired by God's Holy Spirit.

Consequently we have put together a **flexible curriculum,** designed both for correspondence students and campuses, which is a strategy to reach the distant learner; whether provincial, national or international. In fact we have many correspondence students from around the world, including a growing number of successful campuses, in various countries.

This is a growing platform, where men and women of dignity and passion, can grow and be established in their God given endeavours. As God is the healer of the nations, we pray and believe that many of our alumni will go on to **become world changers** in their own right.

We are proud of each and every one of our LICU students.
It would be our pleasure if you would join them on this incredible journey!

Doctor Alan Pateman

Alan Pateman Prof. Ph.D., D.Min., D.D., M.A., B.Th.
PRESIDENT AND CEO
www.licuuniversity.com www.cfeapostolicnetwork.com
Email: info@licuuniversity.com   Mob: +39 366 329 1315

For more information visit our website/facebook or contact our office, using the details below:

Website: www.licuuniversity.com
Facebook: www.facebook.com/LICUMainCampus
Email: info@licuuniversity.com
Telephone: +39 366 329 1315

Alan Pateman Ministries
Presents

Conference

CONNECTING FOR
EXCELLENCE Lucca Italy

An international apostolic and prophetic network

YOUR HOSTS: ALAN PATEMAN   JENNIFER PATEMAN

Please contact our office or download the registration form.
Registration fee: €40

apostledr@alanpateman.com, Tel. 0039 366 329 1315

WWW.ALANPATEMANMINISTRIES.COM

All Books Available

at

APMI PUBLICATIONS

Email: publications@alanpateman.com
*Also Available from Amazon.com
and other retail outlets.*

*If you purchased this book through Amazon.com
or other and enjoyed reading it, or perhaps one of
my other books, I would be grateful if you could
take a couple of minutes to write a Customer
Review, many thanks.*

www.ingramcontent.com/pod-product-compliance
Lightning Source LLC
Chambersburg PA
CBHW071535040426
42452CB00008B/1024